REFLECTIONS OF HOSTILE REVELRIES

REFLECTIONS OF HOSTILE REVELRIES

A COLLECTION OF POLITICAL POETRY MUSINGS
BY JENNIFER C. WOLFE

BLAZEVOX[BOOKS]
Buffalo, New York

Reflections of Hostile Revelries By Jennifer C. Wolfe

Printed in the United States of America

Interior design and typesetting by Geoffrey Gatza
ISBN Number: 978-1-60964-152-8
LOC Number: incoming 2013942418
First Edition

BlazeVOX [books]
131 Euclid Ave
Kenmore, NY 14217
Editor@blazevox.org

publisher of weird little books

BlazeVOX [books]

blazevox.org

21 20 19 18 17 16 15 14 13 12 01 02 03 04 05 06 07 08 09 10

BlazeVOX

Acknowledgements

The author would like to gratefully thank the following sources and individuals for their invaluable contribution to this poetry manuscript:

Geoffrey Gatza, publisher at BlazeVox Books located in Buffalo, New York, for continuing to support my poetry writing and bestowing me with multiple publishing opportunities.

Susan Ricci, the greatest champion of my writing endeavors.

To Mike Heim
Business Management instructor at Century College, White Bear Lake, MN;
A good mentor, teacher, and respected father figure.

Table of Contents

REFLECTIONS OF HOSTILE REVELRIES

Pork Rinds-R-Us

New Jersey's portly GOP Governor, Chris Christie:
That loud-mouthed, glaringly opinionated conservative mouthpiece,
With a girth that dwarfs most public speaking podiums.

Governor Christie is fiercely unapologetic, as to his 276 pound weight,
Grossly disproportionate for his five feet, ten inch height; stating with
Bravado that only his detractors focus on his gigantic bodily frame.

Governor Christie gleefully purports: "I have no thyroid problems; I am not diabetic.
The reason I weigh what I do, is due to eating high fat, high caloric foods;
And as much of them as I can get my hands on."

When asked if he intended to curb his high-fat dietary intake,
Governor Christie, indignant, responded with these words of wit and candor:
"I'm going to eat what I want and as much of it as I want."

OK—and this is supposed to be comforting, to his New Jersey constituency:
That the leader of their state does not have appropriate self-control, or willingly
Chooses to ignore it; deciding to laugh off his obesity as a trivial matter?

The rabid conservative GOP base enjoys highlighting "moral character";
Well, my question for them would be: How does this assessment square
With their mammoth New Jersey Governor, who flaunts the fact that he
Could care less about being obese and will simply continue to "eat what he wants?"

If a Republican Governor willingly shrugs off concern for his health, his
Self-image and his dignity (which, in case he had forgotten, is a reflection upon
The state he governs); perhaps his "moral character" is not as iconic as is heralded.

This from a Governor who uses state police helicopters to transport him to his
Son's sporting events, on the New Jersey taxpayer's dime; so I suppose we really
Should not be surprised at the transmogrification of "moral character" into
"Moral turpentine."

⁖⁗⁐

America's Toughest Sheriff

Ah, Arizona Sheriff, Joe Arpaio; that lovable (not) law enforcement official,
Who delights in throwing any and all Latinos he encounters into his
Widely-hyped network of desert concentration camps. He showcases his
Prisoners via highly-visible roadside chain gangs—and not just the men.
Women and children have their own chain gangs, too. And after a long day
Of removing roadside waste, they return to their flimsy bunk beds inside flapping
Plastic tarpaulin tents, surrounded by fences with guard towers and razor wire.

Yes, Arizona Sheriff, Joe Arpaio, that antagonistic front man for unapologetic
"Discipline," insisting that any and all Latinos he encounters be thrust into his
Concentration camp network, due to their not having their "paperwork" in order.
(That's their "legal" US citizenship paperwork, in case you were wondering).
In Sheriff Arpaio's world, the guise of preventing illegal immigration trumps
ANY Latino person's rights—including those legally residing in the US.

Oh, Arizona Sheriff, Joe Arpaio, that disgruntled buffoon, who grins demonically
Into the nearest TV camera lens, pontificating that: "Everything he does, he does
For the safety of Arizona's 'legal' state populace"—that same populace, which is
Being undermined and otherwise ruined, due to illegal immigrants greedily
Snatching up the low-paying jobs they, themselves, scorn. (Never mind those
AZ businesses that flagrantly and consistently hire illegal workers).

Arizona Sheriff, Joe Arpaio has been christened by fawning GOP acolytes as
"America's toughest sheriff." I heartily agree—in the sense of his being the
Toughest piece of cow manure one has ever attempted to scrape off of the bottom
Of their unfortunate desert cowboy boot. But he needn't worry about his job
Security, or about the derogatory attention he garners; GOP Arizona Governor,
Jan Brewer will be there, to prop him up and to smilingly bolster his derisive tactics.

∞

Pardon Me

Outgoing GOP Mississippi Governor, Hayley Barbour,
You remember him, right? The official who widely touted racist
"Citizen Councils" as the answer to the Ku Klux Klan problem;
And insultingly capitalized upon the unfortunate African-American
Scott sisters' justice bereft incarceration plight, by issuing them a
Stringently-controlled, multi-strings-attached "parole" from prison.

Well, it appears ex-Governor Barbour is up to his faux "magnanimous"
Tricks, once again, in the form of 200 last-minute pardons granted
To convicted murderers, kidnappers, and rapists as he waltzed out
Of the Governor's mansion—in effect, a "Toodle-loo; I'm the Governor,
And I can do anything I want" vein of thinking. "Why, the four murderers
I pardoned were trustees at my mansion," he elaborates, grinning. "I trusted
My grandchildren being around these men; and I would never pardon any
Convict I did not trust my grandchildren being around."

He's kidding, right? Even the basest, most non-reformed inmate serving as a trustee
At the Governor's mansion knows better than to express anything other than
Complete loving stewardship of the man who could grant them a pardon's
Cherubic grandchildren. Does Mr. Barbour really believe that ANY convict
Privileged to work on his mansion's detail would showcase ANYTHING
Other than the "Yes, sir; no, sir, Mr. Governor" rhetoric he is so enamored of?

And so, we have the African-American Scott sisters—two women never
Realistically proven to have participated in the crime for which they were
Incarcerated—that of stealing eleven dollars. And these women were only
Grudgingly "paroled," with their criminal records intact, on the promise that one would
Provide a life-saving kidney transplant for the other. Then, we have four high-profile
Murderers, serving life sentences; that are smilingly "pardoned," their criminal records
Expunged, after working as trustees at the Governor's mansion?

Apparently, in Hayley Barbour's world, murderous "crimes of passion" are
One-time only criminal acts—why everyone knows once they "get their angry
Frustration out of their system," they won't harm anyone again. I beg to point out,
A jury of their peers did not think so; but then their decision and a federal
Mississippi judge's sentencing means nothing to a spitefully biased outgoing
GOP Governor, gleefully stretching his gubernatorial power to the last-minute limit.

80G3

How to Make a Rick Santorum Sweater Vest

Begin with an ordinary long-sleeved wool sweater;
Cut off one arm of self-gratuitous earmark hoarding—translating into
GOP Pennsylvania pet projects which make Mr. Santorum look good;
Next, cut off the second arm of self-gratuitous pork barrel spending—translating into
GOP Pennsylvania pet projects which make the Republican Party look good;
Finish by converting the rounded, common sense collar into an arrogant, uncaring
V-neck, showcasing rabidly conservative ideology, at its lurid finest:

Now you have a Rick Santorum sweater vest you can be proud of.

ಬೃೞ

Fig Newton

Newt Gingrich:
That smugly grinning rake, who imagines himself a "ladies man",
Never mind that he left two wives, while they lay sick.

Newt Gingrich:
That pretentious, smilingly loving "one-woman man",
Now that he has his third pasty blonde, stick figure wife by his side.

Newt Gingrich:
That sensationalized supporter of the "anti-adultery" pledge,
Never mind the complete hypocrisy of his endorsement.

Newt Gingrich:
That (so-called) Washington D.C. "outsider",
Never mind a storied lifetime spent in state and national politics.

Newt Gingrich:
That falsely-heralded "Reagan Republican",
Never mind that Reagan would (and did) eye him scornfully.

Newt Gingrich:
That slickly hyped, pre-packaged image of faux conservatism,
Never mind a bigoted, self-centered voting record.

Newt Gingrich:
That professed man of "impeccable" ethics,
Never mind his censure for outrageous ethical violations.

Newt Gingrich:
That embarrassing stain on the luminous GOP fabric,
Never mind his assertion(s) that he is the savior of the Republican Party.

80C3

Die Hard

Ah, Texas Congressman and repeat Presidential candidate, Ron Paul:
He prances about the political landscape like a zany Warner Brothers cartoon;
A geriatric, "Pepe Le Pew" skunk, foisting bouquets of unrequited flowers
On the moderate GOP base, who are horrified at his lunatic fringe statements.
Why, to hear Mr. Paul tell it—Americans who disagree with the (US) government
Will be forcibly rounded up and herded into concentration camps; minority "animals"
Are on the way to destroy the entire white race, while the US Fed should be
Abolished and the national populace can go back to the barter system,
Trading pots and chickens for goods and services.

In Mr. Paul's contrived, Texas-influenced world, redneck males command their
Homes with an iron fist, subservient wives cater to their husband (or is it their
Dictator's) every whim, everyone owns and shoots fully-automatic AK-47s,
And the Alamo is celebrated as the new American White House.
Yet what is truly amazing about Congressman Paul's incendiary viewpoints,
Is that he never diminishes, in his tenaciously paranoid support of them.
Ever-ready to point out impending US Apocalyptic doom, Mr. Paul races about
The landscape—a raving Jack Nicholson expression from the horror film, "The Shining"
Across his face—while his wide-eyed GOP colleagues stare at him with their
Political mouths agape.

୨୦୯୫

Flippity-Floppity, Romney's on His Way

Mitt Romney is galvanizing his supporters across America, as he plays up
His (alleged) "political prowess" to the American populace.
He darts about the landscape, pausing just long enough to elaborate why
A wealthy millionaire is the individual best-suited to represent
The hardworking, blue collar middle class masses.

Mitt Romney touts his proudly-held political stances, which equate to
Whatever platform or grouping he seeks a political endorsement from:
Cases in point—he was FOR welfare reform, before he was AGAINST it;
He was PRO-CHOICE, before he was PRO-LIFE; and he is the author of
A controversial Massachusetts health-care law that the Obama Administration
Based some of its tenets upon, in their national health care "mandate."
(The SAME health care plan he despises and promises to repeal).

It would seem Mr. Romney has flip-flopped so many times, on so many
Political fronts, that he is in dire need of a permanent, finely-groomed
White sand beach or a luxurious country club swimming pool setting.
(The SAME places most Americans either cannot afford or can only
Visit once-a-year, on their "watch-their-pennies" family vacation).

80CB

Sarah Palin, Presidential Footnote

Ah, Sarah Palin—that loudly opinionated Alaskan GOP mouthpiece
We all know and love. She emerges from the frozen shadows,
To elaborate on what "she" thinks would be in the best interests
Of the GOP; whether it be promoting the destruction of the ANWR
("Drill, baby, drill!") or what powder keg political issue(s) the Republican
Party should focus upon (no new taxes, EVER).

Yes, Sarah Palin—she moves strategically about the US landscape,
Heralding "her" unique political viewpoints with the fanaticism of a
Wild-eyed town crier; glamorously noting that everyone should pay
Attention to HER, because SHE is an all-seeing oracle, whose support
Will make or break any GOP candidate's success.

Please! Is she actually serious? While Ms. Palin does command a
Frighteningly large segment of the extreme right and rabid Tea Party
Segment of the US populace; she holds no lasting political sway
Over the moderate Republican base, whose attention she garners,
With the short-lived life-span of a pesky fruit fly.

My, Sarah Palin—that lackluster political asterisk, highlighting an
Even more lackluster political footnote; "her" time in the center
Of the common sense GOP spotlight is definitely over, no matter
What her carefully engineered spin machine hypes or otherwise purports.
Mainstream America can now get on with their lives, without worrying
About Ms. Palin's Dr. Jekyll/Mr. Hyde childish political tirades.

[Insert a knowing smile and a sardonic WINK here]

ೞೞ

A Vulgar Display of Power

Syrian President, Bashar al-Assad smiles for the nearest state-controlled
Media camera lens, as he opines on his brutal military crackdown:

"My people love me—they hold no ill-will in their hearts toward me,
Or my regime's structural stability. They fully support all of my decrees.
Why, these protestors in Homs et al are anti-government militants," he insists.
"We must crush these divisive attitudes that threaten the sanctity and serenity
Of our beloved, justice-overflowing country. These individuals are confused;
We must help them to shape their viewpoints into line with our collective will.
The totality of that will, might seem harsh, but it keeps our country strong."

"Our people need to be protected from Western-oriented influences,
That convince them they are entitled to a 'free society'. They need to be
Watched over and looked after; like sheep who are protected by their
Loving shepherd. We only have our people's best interests at heart,
Even if that means putting a bullet in their heads, to prevent them from
Being brainwashed by this unholy 'Arab spring'."

"The explosive shells we lob incessantly at the cities of Homs and Aleppo
Are for their benefit—once we purge these stubborn locales of their rebellious
Outlooks, we can get back to the business of everyday Syrian life, where people
Have their fill of bread and one disgruntled glance subjects people to the
Kindhearted stewardship of our security ministry. Why, everyone knows
Our security ministry does not torture anyone."

"The security ministry serves a noble purpose—to 'protect' Syrian citizens
Against themselves. Our nation will only remain strong, so long as its
People are of one mind, one attitude, and one accord. Our loving security forces
Accomplish this feat; and when those they have beneficially 'helped' are
Released; they rejoin their (non-victimized) families with a lobotomized
Grin across their blissfully grateful faces."

"No matter what outside nations or organizations purport; these misguided
Protestors are anti-government terrorists, stirred into action by the vile
Propaganda of Western-oriented 'democracy'. 'Freedom' is such an
Overrated concept—a stint with the security ministry will make that
Abundantly clear. Now, let's all go back to our pre-uprising status-quo,
And everything will be idyllic, magnanimous, and wonderful."

"I'm Bashar al-Assad, and (of course) I approved this message."

⚭

Mother Goose

Former US First Lady, Barbara Bush spoke to the 2012 Republican
Presidential race as being "the worst she had ever seen," with regard to the
Hateful, divisive campaign tactics utilized by all of the candidates.

Well, Ms. Bush would know something about hateful, divisive campaign tactics,
Wouldn't she? Her son, George W. Bush waged a disgraceful 2000 smear strategy
Against Republican AZ Senator John McCain, where he suggested the decorated
War veteran had fathered an illegitimate child with a woman of African-American
Descent—just in time for the race-biased South Carolina GOP primary.

And if that was not enough; we have Ms. Bush's husband, George H.W. Bush,
Who organized the most racist, one-sided, Willie Horton "black people are going to
Burst into your homes and rape all of your wives and daughters" anti-Dukakis
Election strategy, vilifying the African-American community, since the Ku Klux Klan
Held their first angry meeting in Pulaski, Tennessee.

And so—I would opine that former US First Lady, Barbara Bush addressing the
Concept of 2012 Republican Presidential campaign tactics as being some of the
"Worst" she had ever seen pales in comparison to the hateful, divisive political
Strategies her cherished family members have unapologetically perpetrated.

ଜଶ

(Radioactive) Tea, Anyone?

Russia's antagonistic front man, Vladimir Putin recently emerged victorious,
In dubious Russian "elections," decried across the entire country as being
Outrageously fraudulent. Having been barred from running for the Russian
Presidency, after serving his previous two-term limit; Mr. Putin simply became
The Prime Minister "power-behind-the-throne" of President Dmitry Medvedev.

After Medvedev's figure head, one-term Presidential tenure expired, Mr. Putin
Roared back onto the Russian Presidential stage; eagerly propelling himself
Forward, to seek a new term—due to the Russians' lack of foresight, in
Eliminating the "sit-out-the-presidency-for-one-term-and-you-can-run-again"
Political loophole. (Thankfully, the US took care of this conundrum).

So we now, once again, have "President" Putin—the coldblooded tyrant,
Whose "new incarnation" KGB forces shoot inquisitive journalists dead, while
Rounding up any anti-Putin sympathizers into dimly lit prisons, to be unmercifully
Tortured. (This is, by the way, before they are dispatched to the infamous,
Allegedly discontinued Soviet "Gulag" prison system).

But let's not forget about Mr. Putin's most heartless claim to fame:
The ex-KGB agent, living in London, who was poisoned with radioactive
Polonium-mixed hot tea, on his (Putin's) orders. Or that this murderous action
Was prompted by the ex-agent's defection to Great Britain, along with the
Derisive details he exposed, regarding Mr. Putin's favored "Soviet" philosophy.

Remember, Mr. Putin is the man George W. Bush praised, swearing he had
"Looked into his (Putin's) eyes and seen into his soul." What was that "soul"
President Bush is supposed to have seen, I wonder? The faux concerned
Spirit of a man determined to better his once-Communistic country; or was poor
George W. duped by a reprehensible thug, expressing a strategically "positive"
Attitude toward US-Russian political relations?

Yes, Russia's antagonistic front man, Vladimir Putin recently emerged victorious,
In dubious Russian "elections," decried across the entire country as being
Outrageously fraudulent. The pro-Putin Russian political establishment can
Congratulate themselves on setting the progress of their nation back as severely
As when Josef Stalin came to absolute power.

[Having written this poem, your mild-mannered author will now be extremely wary
Of any and all incoming hot tea]

୫୬୯

Murky

US President Barack Obama campaigned in the 2008 general election,
On the precedent of the complete "transparency" of his administration.
Yet scarcely three years later (2011); it was revealed that key members of
His cabinet held weekly meetings away from the White House, at a local
Washington D.C. coffee shop. No official records were kept of the strategic
Planning sessions—indeed, no notes, of any kind, were scribbled out.
(Where they might become available to the American public).

One has to ask themselves: "How do, for all practical purposes, 'secret'
Administration meetings—disguised as friendly coffee-klatches—make for
Alleged political 'transparency'?" It would seem President Obama has
Taken a page out of the CIA secret meeting(s) playbook; except that the
Commander-in-Chief expressly promised his politics would be transparent,
While the Central Intelligence Agency makes no such boasts. One then has
To wonder—are the coffee and any consumed breakfast pastries charged to
US taxpayers, or are the meetings' costs un-transparent, too?

So much for the illusion of "transparency," right? Apparently, in Mr. Obama's
World, off-the-cuff political dialogue, away from the public spotlight,
Over a cup of Joe works just fine.

ಬಂಛ

Panetta Bread

The Panera® Bread Company is famous for its mouthwatering fresh bread;
Former US Secretary of Defense, Leon Panetta is famous for his idiotic fresh take,
On US foreign policy—most notably, regarding America's relationship with
Its primary ally, the nation of Israel.

How else can one explain Mr. Panetta's decision to verbally "out" Israel's
Intelligence-sensitive decision to use military force in response to Iran's growing
Nuclear threat? Standing at a Pentagon podium, ex-Defense Secretary Panetta,
Glowering, bristled over a specific Israeli airstrike timetable.

For Pete's sake! Why not just give away the EXACT date, time, and minute
Of the confidential action—never mind that it leaves poor Israel with
Embarrassed political egg on their face. In Mr. Panetta's world, if a US ally
Does not react in the fashion it assuages; we'll undermine their contrary
Determinations. (Actually, this is an offshoot of President Obama's world).

In any case—we now have Israel blatantly informing the US that when and if
They launch a pre-emptive military strike against Iran's nuclear facilities;
That they will not give America the customary notification of their decision.
And with departed Secretary Panetta blabbing all of their top secret intentions on national
Television, who can really blame them?

৪০০৪

Signing Off

Conservative blogger and (alleged) "journalist," Andrew Breitbart,
Forty-three, passed away from apparent heart failure, after spending
The evening engrossed in heated political dialogue astride a tavern bar stool.

Mr. Breitbart, of course, is famous for his strategically manipulated
Video feed coverage of USDA employee, Shirley Sherrod, making it
Appear as though Ms. Sherrod was anti-farm subsidies for white farmers.
(This resulted in Ms. Sherrod's job termination, you might recall).

When Mr. Breitbart's video coverage was broadcast, in its entirety,
Without being pieced together in a derogatory montage; the truth of
Ms. Sherrod's NON-biased attitude on farm subsidies was finally revealed.

And the most disturbing aspect of Andrew Breitbart and his incendiary
Commentary, is that he believes it is perfectly OK to pick a person or
An organization apart, with unsupported facts and doctored camera footage.

And now that Mr. Breitbart has met with his unceremonious demise,
All of the rabid neo-con elements come out of the proverbial "woodwork,"
To praise and glamorize his derisive "blogging" as groundbreaking documentary.
(Ann Coulter is one of his biggest supporters—enough said).

They pack the right-wing talk shows, in a show of support for their
Fallen hero, placing him atop a symbolic pedestal which he notably does
Not deserve. "But he's dead, now—so that makes him an icon," they intone.

When I view conservative blogger and (alleged) "journalist," Andrew Breitbart;
I equate his engineered "truth" efforts as mere tabloid fodder, where anyone
Who disagrees with him is made the target of his slander. In his world,
Fairness and decency are taboo and a "story's" news worthiness is measured
By its "liberal" bashing shock value.

And so, the blogging landscape is now left devoid of Andrew Breitbart;
I doubt anyone outside of the FOX NEWS crowd will be particularly saddened.

ഇരുന്ന

Saints or Sinners

It has been painstakingly revealed that the New Orleans Saints football team
Paid out monetary "bounties" to its lineup, in exchange for injury-
Inducing "hits" to opposing team football players. The dollar sums were
Varied, depending upon how much physical damage was wreaked
Upon the players' bodies. ($1000 for a bone crushing hit; $1500, if the
Player was knocked out).

"Football is a violent sport," Saints' representatives vociferously argue,
And they are correct. Where their correctness fades; however, lies in
The principle of deliberately inflicting bodily harm. We all know that
Football is a violent sport and that injuries will undoubtedly arise.
But those injuries are not supposed to be premeditated—and while
Agitated team members kneel beside their targeted teammates, praying
That they will be alright; we have the Saints being openly rewarded
For actions which taint football as gladiatorial blood sport.

Here's a playing strategy the Saints' coaching staff might try:
Stop rewarding blatantly un-sportsman-like conduct—and when you
Do get caught, red-faced and embarrassed by sports media outlets
Seizing upon your sordid practices; have something more noble and/or
Apologetic to say, other than: "Football is a violent sport."

80C3

Rush Foot into Mouth

Once again, rabid GOP front man and talk-radio host, Rush Limbaugh roars into the Derogatory spotlight, after criticizing Sandra Fluke, the lone female representative Testifying before a US Congressional panel's analysis of contraceptive coverage. President Obama's administration crafted a controversial tenet of its controversial "Affordable Health Care" law, which requires religious workplaces to cover all Contraception options for its employees—regardless as to whether or not the use of Contraceptives runs contrary to their religious beliefs.

Ms. Fluke, a Georgetown University student, appeared before the panel, merely to Make a case for women's health issues; of which, like it or not, contraception plays a Part. She did not elaborate on having unfettered access to the neocon-despised "Morning After" pill, to prevent unwanted pregnancy—even though this same Medication is a hospital staple given to women who have been sexually assaulted. She also did not advocate for contraceptive health coverage to be mandated, due to Openly suggesting sexual encounters be perpetrated with lustful abandon.

Ms. Fluke simply spoke to the plight of poor or otherwise underprivileged women, Who are unable to afford contraceptives and the effect this might pose to their overall Health. Enter Rush Limbaugh into the sensationalized political fray, galvanizing his Hordes of faithful listeners to ostracize Ms. Fluke as a "slut" and/or a "prostitute." Mr. Limbaugh spitefully remarked further: "If she (Ms. Fluke) wants US taxpayers to Pay for her to have sex; then we want to have something to show for it. Let's make Her stream her sexual trysts, online, so that we can all watch."

I must admit, I am a bit confused as to how advocating for women's health issues Equates to Ms. Fluke wanting US taxpayers to pay for her to have sex? But then, in Rush Limbaugh's narcissistic, self-enshrined world; whatever HE interprets to be the Truth is propelled AS the truth—where he gloats over his (supposed) cleverness, And basks in the glow of his high-five, angry listening audience. On this occasion; However, Mr. Limbaugh may have outdone himself. Eight (and counting) program Sponsors have dropped their financial support of his radio "power hour," while at Least two radio stations have dropped his show from their programming, altogether.

Indeed, Rush Limbaugh's suggestion that Sandra Fluke—or any woman, for that Matter—record their intimate sexual encounters over the Internet, in the manner Of a lurid pornography website; renders him as a voyeuristic letch, if not A completely out-of-touch sexist, who enjoys denigrating women that do not fit His wholesome, 1950's "June Cleaver" image. If a woman asserts herself, Or otherwise expresses her opinion(s); Limbaugh is not interested (unless her words Parrot whatever viewpoint he is enamored of). Those women who deviate from his Required expectations garner his hallmark "Femi-nazi" moniker.

I really don't know what everyone is so upset about? If any woman wants to avoid Unwanted or otherwise inconvenient pregnancy; they can stroll into any Planned Parenthood® clinic and grasp a handful of latex condoms for free, leaving their Workplace health insurance companies completely off of the hook.

80CB

Two Mitt Romney Haikus for You

Smiling Mitt Romney:
His "forty-seven percent";
Did not vote for him.

Good old Mitt Romney,
He made thousand dollar bets,
While Bain pink slips flew.

‘’

Not Quite the Offspring

In honor of the hate-filled, vindictive spirit of the 2012 race for the US Presidency,
I would like to present the glowering campaign trail, at times referred to as the
"Race to the Bottom", as expressed by a variant of a popular alternative rock song:

"Like the latest passion,
Like a spreading unease,
GOPs are bullying, up at the podium,
Trading verbal barbs with the greatest of ease:"

"The PACs stake out their own campaign trails,
You get in their way, and it's all over, pal,
If one guy's slogans and the others don't mix,
They're gonna' smash it up, smash it up, smash it up, smash it up:"

"Hey!
Man, you talkin' back to me?
Take him out!
(You gotta' keep em' separated)"

"Hey!
Man, you disrespecting me?
Take him out!
(You gotta' keep em' separated)"

"Hey!
Don't pay no mind,
You're on the campaign trail, won't be doing any time;
Hey—come out and play!"

[And they say vitriol has gone by the wayside]

৪০৫৪

Video Games

Courtesy of the US Supreme Court, we now have any and all manner of Super
Political Action Committees—known in shortened political slang as "PACS."
Thanks to the high court's landmark ruling; these PACS may contribute unlimited
Amounts of money to a designated candidate's political campaign—while not being
Required to identify themselves as the monetary donors.

And so, in effect, we have millionaire campaign "investors," for all practical
Purposes, "buying" political election slots. (This is hardly a new concept; unions
Across America embraced this strategy, long before it became legalized). But
Thanks to our conservative majority on the Supreme Court, Super PACS have
Emerged as a dynamic, mud-slinging force in steering US election politics.

To me, Super PACs are like 1980's video games at an arcade—I like to
Reference it as a "Super Pac-Man" derivative. You have whatever candidate
Is being supported by their sugar-daddy PAC—and they turn into the cartoon
"Pac-Man," gobbling up lighted dots on their way to politically devouring
Their competing party opponents and colleagues, alike.

"Ah, Super PACS...you gotta' love em'," purports the five member neocon majority
Of the US Supreme Court. I beg to differ with that rosy assessment. The high court's
Tacit approval of political campaigns being "legally" bought and paid for, only
Showcases the principle of "Whoever-has-the-most-money-gets-whatever-they-want,"
At its sordid finest.

Pac-Man and Ms. Pac-Man would be horrified.

೩೦೧೩

Bizarre Ambitions

Recently, cable television guru and Minnesota native, Andrew Zimmern, expressed
A desire to enter into the elected political fray. Apparently, he feels his experience
As the Travel Channel's host of "Bizarre Foods" has prepared him for a foray into
The heated political arena. I think he might be on to something—I mean, politics,
After all, is one of the most "bizarre" realms one may find themselves in, is it not?

The only words of caution I might impart to the intrepid Mr. Zimmern would be to
Tread political waters carefully. Politics is not a plate of food you can simply push
Away, if you do not like what you have been served—it is like an hours derv one
Needs to chew well, before swallowing, or else it will become dangerously lodged
In one's throat and fatally choke off their airway.

Mr. Zimmern purports that he is going to "start small," politically; as in a spot on
His educational district's school board or a seat on his neighborhood City Council.
I think that is a wise choice, on his part. Mr. Zimmern, at least, seems to truly
Want to better his community, as opposed to those narcissistic individuals in love
With the sound of their own school board or City Council voices.

80CB

Mr. Rubio Evokes Little Havana

You remember freshman Florida Tea Party Senator, Marco Rubio, right?
The politician who claims to speak with complete authority on the plight of
US soldiers serving in Afghanistan, due to his one-time, VIP visit to the region?
Well, recently Mr. Rubio was up to his faux antics, once again, elaborating on
How his family fled from Cuba to America, as a result of Fidel Castro assuming
Power. He tearfully appeared before media cameras, to highlight himself and
His family members as being political refugees, fleeing a totalitarian state.

It's too bad that Mr. Rubio's crocodile tear allegations are totally FALSE;
(His family emigrated to America in the 1950's BEFORE Castro came to power in Cuba).
Senator tea pot was merely playing to the vast Cuban-American community located
Within Miami's famous "Little Havana," who have no time for either Fidel Castro,
Or for false impersonators claiming to identify with their authentic political persecution.
When he was questioned about his "fleeing-for-their-lives" family boasts; Mr. Rubio
Complained that he would have to "research his family history more fully."

Rubio made no apologies for his non-credible assertions—instead, blaming the (allegedly)
"Anti-right-wing" media establishment for his problematic scrutiny. Please!
Senator Rubio simply got caught with his political pants down; and wants to blame anyone
Other than himself for emphatically speaking before carefully thinking. Instead of
Weighing the gravity of what he was saying, he opened his rabidly conservative mouth
And inserted his decidedly less-than-honest Tea Party foot. And no matter what he or
His political camp purport; no amount of backtracking will erase the ramifications of
Pretending to be a penniless Cuban refugee—when in reality, your upper middle class
Family sought a new life in America, to expand their monetary and political fortunes.

Back to the drawing board, for garnering Little Havana's voter support, it would seem.

৵ৎৎ

Stomp

Minnesota's DFL Governor, Mark Dayton blatantly informed proponents of a
New MN Vikings football stadium that the chosen site would have to be atop the
Exact same location the current collapsible Metrodome occupies, or no state
Taxpayer funding would be allotted for the building process.

Even though a much more consumer-friendly locale is situated in Arden Hills,
Governor Dayton nixed the prospective site, due to a proposed .01 percent tax
Increase, which caused Ramsey Country residents to come unglued. And so,
Dayton sallies forth, issuing his ultimatum to Vikings' owner, Zygi Wilf that to
The immediate left of the original Metrodome is where a new stadium will go.

If I were Mr. Wilf, I might have been tempted to turn the Governor down and
Move the team to a plethora of other states that had no problem with building
Expansive stadiums on sites the Vikings were actually interested in. Thankfully,
However, Mr. Wilf agreed to keep the beloved Vikings in their beloved home state;
Even though it meant acquiescing to Governor Dayton's funding ultimatum.

Next, our intrepid Governor informed MN Congresswoman, Michele Bachmann
That she would either need to get behind a workable plan for a new Stillwater
Lift bridge or face its already-allotted MN DOT funding being allocated to "other"
Projects. Now—while I have no problem with Governor Dayton putting Michele
Bachmann in her legislative place; I do have a problem with his condescending
"My way or the highway" gubernatorial attitude.

I must have missed that part in the Minnesota Constitution, where the governor
Was declared absolute sovereign.

ಬಿಂಬ

Michele Bachmann Rides Again (and Away)

Fresh from her failed attempt to garner the 2012 GOP US Presidential
Nomination; MN Congresswoman, Michele Bachmann boisterously thrust
Herself back into the sixth district, Land-of-10,000-Lakes Washington D.C. fray.
(Not mentioning the fact that the MN GOP-controlled state legislature strategically
"Re-districted" her political area, to ensure that she would win national political
Re-election—had she been positioned to run against her rightful DFL challenger,
Minnesotans would finally have been rid of her).

But, I digress.

And so, Michele Bachmann, that deer-in-the-headlights facial expression,
Tea Party Caucus mouthpiece we all know and love returned to her faux "home" state
(Remember, she is a gleeful Iowa native); where she celebrated returning to her
MN Congressional duties and on how "positive" she felt, to be back. If I might
Address her simpering, vapid smile-on-a-stick approach to her constituency;
I would point out that her continued presence on the national political scene equates
To a mud stain which no amount of detergent will remove from the MN table cloth.

But then, the most astonishing event occurred—Ms. Bachmann removed herself from
The national political scene, announcing she would not seek US Congressional re-election:
This decision brought forward, incidentally, on the heels of the FBI announcing its
Investigation into finance discrepancies associated with her 2012 US Presidential campaign.
With her unexpected and highly celebrated political departure; the mud stain on the
Minnesota tablecloth has faded into that one stubborn defacing mark, which remains a
Casual reminder of a chagrined annoyance that has left its permanent disgruntled mark.

కంస

Tortoise Newt – A Haiku for You

Newt is a turtle,
And just like a turtle's shell,
Newt carries baggage.

౩౦౮

Killing, Inc.

US Attorney General, Eric Holder recently announced the policy that
President Obama holds the authority to designate American-born citizens
As "terrorists" and to that end, have them assassinated—IF it has been
Determined that they are a threat to US "National Security," that is.

"The 'War on Terror' gives the President universal power to protect
American interests against rogue individuals who join Al-Qaeda or enlist
In Islamic Fundamentalist jihad," Holder elaborates. The disturbing
Conundrum in all of this; however, lies in the precedent of US rule-of-law.

US rule-of-law, under the US Constitution, allows for US citizens to be
Afforded a trial by a jury of their US peers, for any crimes that they might
Have committed (War on Terror actions included). It does NOT allow for
US citizens to be actively gunned down, without trial or even arrest.

Murdering individuals who act against their governments, and justifying
It under the guise of ensuring "National Security," is a strategy that American
Foes have exercised for many years. And so, the US President may now
Taint their hands with their citizens' blood as effortlessly as Vladimir Putin.

Like it or not, US citizens do NOT divorce themselves from American justice
Or rule-of-law, due to fighting as an Islamic extremist against the US Government.
American Taliban, John Walker was arrested and sent to Guantanamo, to undergo
US military tribunal—he was not arbitrarily shot dead on the battlefield.

The President and Mr. Holder, it would seem, prefer a policy immortalized by a
Platinum-selling album title from heavy metal icons, Megadeth: "Killing is my business;
And business is good." And since their "Fast & Furious" strategy to track weapons
Provided to Mexican drug cartels proved so amazingly "successful," (complete with
The deaths of two US border patrol agents) should we really be surprised?

ಬಿಂಣ

Flashpoint

In the middle of the night (actually early morning), a US soldier left his military
Base in Afghanistan, made his way to two neighboring Afghan villages, and
Calmly massacred sixteen Afghan civilians. Some of the dead were yanked
By their hair into open doorways; others were simply shot within the interiors
Of their homes. Villager eyewitnesses insist there was more than one soldier
Participating in the gruesome melee—the US military insists otherwise.

"This unfortunate instance was the work of one soldier," they maintain,
Perpetrating the "lone gunman" theory, which has been utilized to calm the
Concerned American masses, from the days of the John F. Kennedy assassination
Until the present. They do not elaborate upon the Staff Sergeant in-question
Having been trained as a US Special Forces operative, where "kill" operations
Are commonplace and induce as much ethical concern as swatting at a fly.
US Pentagon officials also refuse to comment on the sergeant's three previous
Tours in Iraq or what function he performed, while serving there.

And so, there is little to go on, as to why a seasoned US military veteran would
Leave his base to murder Afghan villagers, on his very first Afghan deployment?
I suppose the horrors experienced in fighting a war based on lies (Iraq) have nothing
To do with it? Or the intense pressure American military forces are under, to make
President Obama's Afghanistan War "surge" appear needed and successful?
("Of course not," Pentagon officials dutifully intone. "And you—meaning your
Mild-mannered author—are 'unpatriotic' to even suggest such scenarios.").

In the words of today's casual youth: "Whatever."

Afghan President, Hamid Karzai wants the sergeant publicly tried in Afghan courts,
To serve as a lesson in deterrence against other US soldiers committing atrocities.
If I were he, I would not hold my breath for THAT to occur. "Unforgivable" offenses
Perpetrated by US military personnel stationed within occupied countries, stay within
The US military court system—where the perpetrators usually serve three to ten years
In a military prison, along with being dishonorably discharged.

(Sort of a Las Vegas "What Happens in Afghanistan stays in the US" vein of thinking).

೧೦೭೫

Danger, Will Robinson!

What is a GOP "Robo" call, you might ask? They are incessantly annoying
Automated telephone calls incessantly imploring prospective voters to endorse
Incessantly annoying political candidates—Michele Bachmann, for example.

As for myself, hearing a robotic GOP voice enticing me to cast my "independent"
Vote for the Robo-call's selected candidate-of-choice hardly inspires any
Positive voting reply; other than annoyed candidate dismissal and/or disdain.

I only wish that ordinary voters could turn the tables on political
Candidates, and blanket them with nauseating "Robo-calls."
Mine might sound something like this:

"Hello, Jane Q. Voter, here—and if Republicans think their allegedly clever
'Robo' calls to my home phone are going to garner them my 'Independent' voter
Support; then I would like to suggest both they and their automated switchboard go
Jump into the nearest lake—Minnesota has 10,000 of them, you know."

80G3

The Gift that Keeps on Giving

Texas Congressman and repeat US Presidential candidate, Ron Paul
Has a problem—a doggedly tenacious problem—personified in the Libertarian
Newsletter that bears his name.

Texas Congressman and repeat US Presidential candidate, Ron Paul's
Newsletter sparks heated political controversy, due to the inflammatory content
It freely dispenses to its (allegedly) discerning reading audience.

Let's analyze some of the Ron Paul Newsletter's insightful comments, shall we?

"If you have ever been robbed by a black, teenaged male; you know how
Unbelievably fleet-footed they can be." (1992)

"By far, the most powerful lobby in Washington, of the bad sort, is the Israeli
Government." (2008)

"Given the inefficiencies of what (Washington) D.C. calls the 'criminal justice
System,' I think we can safely assume 95 percent of black males in that city
Are criminals." (1992)

Texas Congressman and repeat US Presidential candidate, Ron Paul states
That "he" does not write the articles presented within his newsletter, nor does
Mr. Paul elaborate upon what individual does write them.

Texas Congressman and repeat US Presidential candidate, Ron Paul then insists
That the content of his newsletters should not matter to prospective voters who
Are vacillating on committing their support to him—He is their man.

I beg to differ with Mr. Paul—if he cannot keep track of, or bother to be informed
On, his newsletters' contents, it causes me to wonder exactly how many OTHER
Proverbial skeletons are hidden inside his political closet, waiting to emerge?

Texas Congressman and repeat US Presidential candidate, Ron Paul reacts
Defensively, when questioned about the articles showcased within his newsletter.
He angrily stalks out of media interviews, in response to their scrutiny.

Lastly, Texas Congressman and repeat US Presidential candidate, Ron Paul relates that He will drop out of politics, should his FOURTH drive for the US Presidency be Unsuccessful, retiring after thirty-six years spent in TX Washington D.C. politics.

(A more poignant argument for US Congressional term-limits, stemming from Mr. Paul and his offensive newsletter, you would be hard-pressed to find).

೮ಜ

Enter the Dragon Lady

Home Box Office (HBO) aired a controversial TV movie on the
2008 John McCain-Sarah Palin drive for the US White House entitled:
"Game Change." The movie, based upon the first-hand accounts of
Campaign happenings, as chronicled in the non-fiction book, *Game Change*,
By authors John Heilemann and Mark Halperin, walks the American public
Through the sixty-days of AZ GOP Senator, John McCain's Presidential foray,
From the moment he announced Alaska Governor, Sarah Palin as his Vice Presidential
Running mate, until the November general election, which he lost to Barack Obama.

From the onset, HBO producers faced heavy criticism from the rabid neo-con front,
Outraged that the movie laid all of Mr. McCain and Ms. Palin's embarrassing foibles
Bare, for US television audiences to see and snicker at. And no one levied the harshest
Derisive commentary on the film, other than Sarah Palin, herself—who even released a
Specialized series of You Tube videos to refute the TV film as being (among other things)
"Blatantly pro-liberal." I find it tedious how the ultra-rabid conservative GOP front
Accuses ANY avenue which portrays them in an unflattering light as being engineered
By the pesky "liberal machine"—which, apparently has nothing better to do, than to
Find and seize upon opportunities to make them (the GOP) look bad.

And "Game Change," by the way, DOES succeed in finding a great many aspects
Revolving around the 2008 McCain-Palin campaign, which DOES make their
Political strategy legitimately look bad, ranging from Senator McCain's decision to
Select Ms. Palin, courting the feminine vote so enamored of Hillary Clinton,
To Palin's disastrous television interviews, where she boasted that she could
Physically see Russia from her Wasilla, Alaska homestead—so that rendered her as
Being well-versed in US foreign policy. (And this is AFTER the viewing audience
Has seen her frenetically scribbling uninformed crib notes on Adolph Hitler's Germany
Being the primary anti-US aggressor in World War II).

For all of Ms. Palin's outrage; however, she cannot erase the fact that the material
Showcased within "Game Change" comes directly from the McCain-Palin political
Staffers who witnessed their hard-fought campaign implode, first-hand. What?
Are they ALL lying or making false statements, simply to "smear" her already stained
Political reputation? Are they expressing "sour grapes" sympathies, over their assessment
That "she" single-handedly sank their Presidential campaign against Barack Obama?
Please! Most any (non-GOP) person who views the 2008 McCain-Palin campaign
With a truthfully discerning political eye, knows that Sarah Palin and her numerous
Embarrassing verbal gaffes, comments, and opinions are EXACTLY what doomed their
Quest for the US White House (where polls showed Senator McCain EVEN with
A virtually unknown Mr. Obama, prior to selecting Palin as his VP).

Here is a little bit of candor for Ms. Palin to consider:

Just because "she" refutes the disparaging political events she has been embroiled in,
As being untrue does not make them untrue. And as to Senator McCain's public
Statement: "Of course, I have no plans to watch 'Game Change'," I do not blame
Him—as the film clearly demonstrates how his opportunistic venture to cater to female
Voters, by thrusting a completely unprepared VP candidate into his campaign spotlight,
Without taking the time to properly vett her qualifications, blew up in his face.

సు◌రి

Go for the Green

In 2009, US President Barack Obama's administration utilized its clout to
Oversee the awarding of a $535 million (that's half a BILLION dollars)
Loan to the Solyndra Corporation, at the forefront of the "green" energy
Solar power industry. The monetary award was meant to spur the concept of
Alternative energy development. (A platform Mr. Obama had campaigned
Heavily on, in the 2008 US Presidential race).

Of the 134 US companies which had applied to the US Department of
Energy's alternative energy "loan guarantee" program; Solyndra was
The first company to receive a multi-million dollar government payout.
Having been plagued by disturbing financial red flags, during the solar panel
Company's vetting process, the Obama Administration pressured the
Dept. of Energy to quickly grant Solyndra the loan, highlighting their plant as
The jewel in Mr. Obama's "green energy" crown.

Not long after President Obama made a smiling public appearance with
Solyndra executives; however, the multi-million dollar loan tapestry his
Administration had woven with the company began to unravel. With the
Dept. of Energy having turned down Solyndra's original loan application in
May of 2008, due to blatant financial solvency worries, media reports began to
Surface about President Obama pressuring energy officials to award the loan in
January of 2009; presumably after determining the corporation was a positive
White House "green energy" political opportunity.

Having promised upwards of 4000 new jobs at their loan-approved solar panel facility,
Solyndra abruptly ceased all of its activities and filed for Chapter 11 bankruptcy
Protection, not only nixing the proposed incoming 4000 jobs, but laying off 1100
More company employees, as well. The *New York Times* reported on the Solyndra
Debacle, demonstrating in exacting detail, not only how the Obama Administration
Had pressured the Dept. of Energy to grant an extremely risky loan, but also their
Reasoning behind doing so—several top Solyndra executives had made substantial
Donations to Mr. Obama's 2008 Presidential campaign.

It should be noted that this is hardly a new concept—think George W. Bush and
Enron or Dick Cheney and Halliburton. What was different and what actually
Hurt; however, was that Mr. Obama was supposed to have been the alternative
To "one-hand-washes-the-other" cash politics. After eight miserable years spent
Under the thumb of George W. Bush et al, America was desperate to move forward,
On a brighter political note and toward a brighter political future. Mr. Obama
Promised that he would be different—that he would be the positive "change"
US citizens were looking and hoping for.

Back to the drawing board for that type of candidate, I guess—or were Americans Simply naïve to entertain the possibility of a real-time "Mr. Smith goes to Washington" scenario?

෩෬

Books, Galore!

These days, it seems that every political person (or non-political person,
For that matter) is releasing their (often ghost) written memoirs. If they do not
Release actual memoirs; they release some other form of written work,
Espousing "their" unique insights on life. I would like to address a few titles
Emanating from the political spectrum and add my return commentary to them:

First, we have "Decision Points" by former US President, George W. Bush.
Within its glistening pages, George W. offers a hopelessly optimistic version of
His eight-year Presidential tenure, criticizing any perceived low points as "the
Left-wing's determination to undermine me."

My response to Mr. Bush's book consists of angry skepticism. George W's
Written "legacy" is NOT some rose-colored glasses stroll down the Bush
Family dynasty memory lane—it is a succession of blunders, inarticulate
Use of the English language, and foreign policy disasters that left America
With its reputation stained on all moral and ethical fronts. (Oh and by the way,
"Dubya" does not need the alleged left-wing to undermine him; he does quite
Well at that, on his own).

Next, we have "In my Time," by ex-Vice President, Dick Cheney, where the
Glowering official who gleefully admits to being the "evil genius in the corner
Who nobody sees," and that that was a "nice way to operate" expounds upon the
"War on Terror," as though it is the greatest invention since sliced bread. He
Defends his US White House connection with Halliburton as being "vital" and he
Vindictively smears any/all detractors as annoying "gnats."

My response to Mr. Cheney's book is one of furious refutation. Dick
Certainly lives up to his first name, roaring across the US Presidential landscape,
Like some lumbering troll engrossed in getting his way, to the exclusion of
Anyone else's ambitions (including George W's). In Dick's world, everything
Is all about him, including the title to his memoir. I agree with the widespread
Assessment that Mr. Cheney is comparable to Star Wars' Darth Vader—except
That in Dick's case, he does not seek any form of palpable redemption. (Oh and if
Mr. Cheney takes offense and wants to come after me, I am afraid I shall have to
Decline any prospective duel invitations, as I've left my light saber at home).

Lastly, we come to that pinnacle of self-centered narcissism, Ann Coulter and
Her book, "If Democrats had any Brains, They'd be Republicans." I am not even
Going to address her non-lucid, anti-DFL ravings, responding to the book with this
Lone observation: "If Ann Coulter had any decency, she would not vilify grieving
9/11 widows as capitalizing upon their husband's deaths."

&⚭&

Keystone Cops

The rabidly conservative GOP made a rabidly conservative mockery of
US President Barack Obama's declination to pursue the proposed "Keystone
Pipeline," an oil pipeline running from Alberta, Canada, to "key" (stone) points
On the Texas Gulf Coast. The construction process for the pipeline consists
Of three major parts, with Phase 1, running from Canada to Nebraska, having
Already been completed and gone online, in June of 2010.

In November of 2011, US Senate Republicans introduced legislation aimed
At forcing President Obama to approve the completion of the Keystone Pipeline,
Within a 60-day timeframe. The Obama Administration refused the ultimatum,
Postponing any decision on the pipeline, until 2013 (conveniently after the 2012
General election). The GOP establishment went into a highly-visible meltdown
Over the decision, decrying Mr. Obama as being "anti-jobs" and longing to
Perpetuate America's dependence upon foreign oil.

If I might address these strategically manipulated GOP "concerns," I would like
To point out that the only tenet of the neo-con crowd, which is even slightly
True, consists of the fact that finishing the pipeline will, indeed, create thousands
Of immediate jobs within the beleaguered US construction industry. What
Republicans do not mention; however, is that these jobs are only TEMPORARY.
When the pipeline's construction is completed, the jobs will evaporate, with only
A minimal staff being kept on, to monitor and control pipeline machinations.
So much for the President "killing" thousands of American jobs—the jobs held a
Limited shelf-life, to begin with.

I would next point out that the GOP's insistence the oil from the Keystone Pipeline
Would bring about American independence from foreign oil is misleading at best,
If not an actual lie, at worst. Top production expectations from the pipeline are
Roughly 500,000 barrels of oil per day—a good chunk of oil from North America,
Yes; but not enough to erase the US' dependence upon foreign oil sources. Indeed,
Several speculative reports show the majority of the oil produced by the pipeline as
Being earmarked for exportation to other countries—so which is it, oil for American
Consumers or oil to be placed on the export auctioning block?

And lastly, I would like to point out that President Obama did NOT nix the pipeline,
Altogether—although with the GOP's derogatory fervor, one would be hard-pressed to
Realize that fact. He simply placed the pipeline on the energy backburner, to further
Determine if its construction was in the country's national "best interest." If you ask me,
What is more in the US' national best interest is for US legislators to stop acting like a
Bunch of kindergarteners throwing a screaming tantrum, if they do not get their way.

80Q3

White House Blues

I had (and still do) have high hopes for US President Barack Obama,
As America's first African-American President and beyond. After two
Terms of George W. Bush being at the national helm, I was as excited as
The next person for a fresh presidential start on a clean presidential slate.
And while Mr. Obama has disappointed on the US economy front, I think
We need to keep in mind the destroyed American economy he first stepped
Into, courtesy of an eight-year George W. financial train wreck.

That being said, I feel I must point out several areas where President Obama
Has disappointed:

After promising to close down the US Naval Prison at Guantanamo Bay, Cuba,
The facility decried by Amnesty International as the "Gulag of our time," still
Remains open—going on four years later. And while I realize it was probably
Naïve, on Mr. Obama's part, to make such a promise (actually not, since it has
Been successfully demonstrated that War on Terror prisoners can be incarcerated
On US soil, with no terror attacks imminent; case in point: the Nigerian Christmas
Airline bomber), a promise is a promise—and this promise has not been kept.

Then, after indicating that the US policy of "extraordinary rendition," (where
America sends its War on Terror captives abroad, to be tortured in fashions that
Would outrage US citizens, if they were conducted on US soil), would be discontinued,
We find the program is still alive and being actively practiced—leading countries who
Look to the US as an example, to believe it is perfectly alright to treat their prisoners
Like inhuman slabs of meat. This was never a promise, but a wonderful hope—and
This hope has now been dashed.

Next, the Obama administration bullied the US Department of Energy into granting
A high-risk loan to a green energy corporation (Solyndra) whose top executives
Had donated large sums of money to Mr. Obama's 2008 US presidential campaign.
(That's half a BILLION dollars awarded to a company, whose worrisome financial
Red flags had prompted its original loan application to be turned down). When the
Company declared Chapter 11 bankruptcy, shortly thereafter, it was like pouring
Financial salt into an open financial wound that might easily have been avoided.
This was a common political occurrence I believed Mr. Obama would not
Have been a party to—and this belief has now been brought down to reality.

Also, after campaigning on the promise that his administration would operate
With complete "transparency," President Obama's advisory team conducted
Off-the-record, strategic planning sessions at a local Washington D.C. coffee
House—where no notes or details of any kind were recorded, lest they come
Under public scrutiny. To me, "transparency" is transparent; it does not skirt
Detection, like a covert CIA operation. This was a promise I was excited that
Mr. Obama made—and this promise has also not been kept.

There are many obstacles that stand in a US President's way, toward their being
An effective leader—made all the more disillusioning, when they, themselves,
Are contributing factors to those obstacles.

෫෬

Pump Up the Incendiary Volume

"Greetings, my fellow Americans! It's nice to be able to talk with you,
Today. Let's jump right in and talk about the pain you are all feeling
At your local gas pump, shall we?"

"The fact that the national average for a gallon of gas is hovering around
$4.00 ($5.00 on select US coasts) is completely President Obama's fault! Why,
If a Republican was the US President, gas prices would lower to $2.50 a gallon."

"President Obama holds absolute sway over the price you pay at the pump!
You better believe he does! He axed the Keystone Pipeline and everyone knows
That the oil derived from that pipeline would equal domestic oil independence."

"President Obama encourages America's reliance upon foreign oil—and never mind
What new "green energy" ideas he advocates. Wind and solar power are for the
Birds—we have all of the oil we need, just over the border in Canada and we can't
Even bring it into our country, courtesy of the Obama Administration."

"So, remember folks—if you want $2.50 gas at the pump, keep the GOP in mind!
Oh and if by some quirk, that promise cannot be delivered on, keep in mind that a
GOP US White House is not in control of oil intake or gasoline refinery production."

[I'm Newt Gingrich—and I approved this message]

৪৩

Delusions of Grandeur

After leaving the 2012 GOP US Presidential race in disgrace, (which he
Animatedly blamed on everyone, other than himself), GOP candidate,
Herman Cain elaborated that "he would be back." "Terminator" fans
Beware, it would seem.

You remember Herman Cain, right? The once regal African-American
US Presidential hopeful, who had never actually held any elected position?
He did have a notable business background, as the CEO of the "Godfather's
Pizza" chain, which he enthusiastically heralded as a beneficial quality,
In tackling the floundering US economy.

Mr. Cain glamorized himself as being the ultimate Washington D.C.
"Outsider," in an effort to court voters disgusted by lackadaisical US
Politicians, submerged in a polarized haze of non-cooperation and
Non-compromise.

It's too bad that Mr. Cain was, instead, glamorized as a randy skirt chaser,
Who used his position of workplace authority to pressure women's
Participation in lurid sexual acts; or even worse, as a pre-cursor to a pretty
Young woman even being offered a job.

The final straw which broke his beleaguered GOP political campaigns' back;
However, was when a long-time Georgia mistress emerged from the shadows,
Showcasing her and Mr. Cain's extramarital relationship on national television.

Through it all, Mr. Cain's longsuffering wife remained loyal to her husband,
Although it is not rumored that she accepted the affair with the same affinity she
Accorded the five (and counting) women who came forward to accuse him of
Sexual harassment. (Where's my Tammy Wynette "Stand by Your Man" 45,
When I need it?).

In a post-campaign CNN interview, Herman Cain promised that he would be a
Dynamic force in US politics, by starting his very own political coalition. He did
Not go into detail about how his coalition would affect political change, but he
Maintained that it definitely would be a political force to be reckoned with.

In the words of today's casual youth: "Yeah, right."

৪৩৪৪

Our Friend, Pakistan

Our friend, Pakistan:

That emerging, want-to-be modernistic marvel of the Islamic-dominated age,
Who desperately tries to have it all; religious-controlled capitalism with
Dogmatically-curtailed freedom.
They arrest individuals who helped the US find and neutralize Osama Bin Laden.
They regularly threaten to nuke neighboring rival and despised archenemy, India.
They take no real effort at ousting anti-US fighters inhabiting their mountain regions.
Their support of American policy endeavors changes at a moment's whim or notice.
If you ask me, the only reason our friend, Pakistan, is our friend at all,
Is that they possess nuclear weapons and the US military needs their tactical proximity
To the region for the success of their war efforts, most notably in Afghanistan.

"What's wrong with that?" the GOP argues. "Our unmanned drones need that
Critical airbase, where we can bomb Taliban resistance pockets with impunity. And if
A few civilians happen to be maimed or killed, that's just collateral damage."

෴

Not So Happy Meals

The State of California has launched into a managed "healthy food"
Initiative, by dictating to the McDonald's Corporation which of their
Iconic children's "happy meals" may include promotional toys or not.

If the happy meal is to be allowed to offer the promotional toy, the meal
Has to meet specific healthy food requirements, which include fruit snacks
And exclude French fries.

If the happy meal does not conform to state-mandated parameters, then the
Promotional toy children are clamoring for, within the meal, will not
Be included for them.

I fail to see where a US state has ANY business, much less the legal right,
To force fast food corporations to comply with their food-sensitive policies.
What's next—seafood restaurants are not allowed to serve fried fish, due to
The high-fat breading? Or maybe steak houses being closed down, in response
To the cholesterol dangers of red meat?

With their economy hovering on the brink of financial default; I think it
Would behoove the State of California to focus on more pressing issues than
Monitoring which McDonald's happy meals are allowed to include toys.

And in answer to the state's "healthy food" directive; I would like to point out,
If your troubled economy was such that people actually derived a decent wage from
Their jobs, perhaps they could afford to eat healthy food, instead of wandering
Into the nearest fast food restaurant to order items off of the high-fat, yet
Pocketbook-friendly "dollar" menu.

⊱⊰

The Problem We all Live With

A high school student walks into a crowded cafeteria, pulls out a gun,
And shoots several of their classmates dead. In fact, it does not necessarily
Need to be within the school's cafeteria; it can be in an interior school hallway.
Or it can be in a school library or a crowded school auditorium—anywhere within
A public or private school may be considered a target area.

Without fail, the number-one reason troubled high school students turn
To violence consists in their being picked on by school bullies. Whether it is a
Derisive sneer, an incendiary remark, or derogatory laughter, bullies single out
Anyone that does not conform to "their" specifications of what or who is "cool."
Also without fail, is that the number-one grouping of high school students who are
Bullies consists of the "popular" kids, who usually rove about in multi-member
Cliques. These "cliques" set the bullying pace.

When students are bullied, to the point of a psychological break; there are two
Ways in which they normally manifest any potential violence. They will either
(a) Kill themselves, due to being unable to cope with the often vicious abuse they
Have been exposed to or (b) They will turn their inner aggression outward, where
They kill the source of their unbearable mistreatment. It has always been amazing
To me, to survey how the popular clique people, touched by the violence of their own
Bullying, are celebrated as icons, while the surrounding community, at-large,
Expresses their eternal sorrow and completely vilifies the bullied student-killer.

While I do NOT support ANY action which resorts to murderous violence; I have
To wonder if the problem(s) might have been averted, by school officials taking a
More serious stance on preventing bullying? (At least, the bullying that occurs on
School grounds or at school-sponsored events). And let's be completely honest,
Here—just because a school bully is killed does not automatically transform
Them into a school hero. They are not heroes—they are bullies; most likely,
Those bullies who go on to become the workplace bosses people love to hate.

School administrators have a critical responsibility to the needs and safety of
Their students. What any student desires is a safe environment to be able to learn in,
Without being labeled as a "fag," a "dyke," a "loser," or a "freak."

ဆဩ

Rampant Rampage

It would appear that people, everywhere, have lost any
Sense of self-control—indeed, any even minor semblance of it.

A sullen youth walking down the street makes eye contact with another
Youth, does not like what they see in their eyes, and whips out a gun.

A rebuffed suitor takes out their unrequited aggression on the individual who,
In their eyes, casually "dismissed" them, by throwing acid in their face.

A man or a woman waiting at a public bus stop decides someone standing
Nearby has "dissed" (i.e. disrespected) them, and punches begin flying.

An upset father, furious over his son's basketball team losing their state
Championship game; angrily bites off his son's coach's ear.

Parents' attending their children's sporting events become enraged at one
Another's support for the opposite team, erupting into violent fisticuffs.

A sexually depraved individual forces their way into an innocent person's life
And brutally rapes them.

A mentally troubled young man places an ad for a babysitter on Craigslist;
Then murders the young woman who shows up to apply for the job in cold blood.

You do not have to go far, to witness that society, at-large, seems to have
Abandoned any pretense at even civility, much less self-control.

What has happened, to bring about this sad state-of-affairs, I often wonder?
Is it the demise of the nuclear family unit? Is it because children are raised in
Abusive households and become abusers, themselves?

There are no easy answers, as to why society has devolved to the point where
One is afraid to make eye contact with, much less smile at a stranger, worried
Over whether or not they will feel belittled and attack them.

I think it all has something to do with the fact that the US has become a violent
"Melting-pot," where individuals want instant gratification in every aspect of their
Lives; feeling that society "owes" them; when in actuality, they owe themselves.

Sigh—and I swore I would never sound like my father.

৪০೦೪

Recipe for Tea Party Three-Layer Cake

Mix one layer of skewed eccentricity;
Mix one layer of egotistical arrogance;
Mix one layer of self-righteous indignation.

Bake at a high-degree of scathing moral outrage,
Directed at anyone and anything that does not agree
With Tea Party dogma, until light and golden.

Frost with plenty of Tea Party condescension.

Serving Size: This cake is for TEA PARTY members only.
Everyone else may direct their attention to the day-old pastry aisle at
The local supermarket.

ട്ടെ ભ

To Fee or not to Fee

Bank of America has been in the news headlines, yet again, in an
Unflattering fashion—however, this time, it was for adding a "fee,"
To customers who wanted to use their Bank of America debit cards.

For merely $5.00 per transaction, Bank of America customers were
Graciously treated to the privilege of utilizing their very own
Bank of America-issued debit cards for consumer purchases.

Debit cards serve a vital consumer purchasing function, as they are
Accepted anywhere a major VISA credit card is; however, they directly
"Debit" money from an individual's checking account, without their
Spending money they do not have or receiving a high-interest credit card bill.

When Bank of America announced its intention to charge its customers
Fees for their debit card usage; it was not well-received. Angry hordes of
Consumers closed out their Bank of America accounts, preferring to take
Their "debit" card business to banking institutions that did not penalize
Their customers for actually using their cards.

In the end, Bank of America pulled an abrupt about-face, with their debit
Card "fee" policy; deciding it was "in the best interest" of their customers,
If they did not charge $5.00 for every debit transaction.

My response to Bank of America is that it was probably not a wise idea to
Charge your customers for simply using the banking tools YOU avail for their
Use and convenience, in the first place, yes? And my, but how magnanimous of
You, to reverse course on your ill-conceived, greedy-for-banking-profits decision.
Would you like for your disgruntled customers to issue you a round of applause?

Now—if I could only find a bank that allows patrons to make cash withdrawals,
At non-banking institution-specific ATM machines, without a fee; life would be perfect.

৪৹੭

TSA Light

The Transportation Safety Administration (TSA) has announced its
New airline screening procedures, addressing America's elderly
Population. It seems that the days of physically running rough shod,
Over wheelchair-bound travelers, resulting in the bursting of an older
Gentleman's colostomy bag which left him sitting in a pool of his
Own urine, are (thankfully) over.

Top TSA officials have "lightened" three primary screening strictures,
Aimed at lessening the humiliation elderly airline passengers endure, for
Whom flying is already an arduous physical burden, made all the more taxing,
By being subjected to pre-flight screening activities. Apparently, older (and
Especially wheelchair-ridden) airline passengers will not be required to remove
Their shoes; they will not be required to remove any light outerwear (i.e. cardigans),
And they will have fewer strenuous physical pat-downs.

I believe these screening allowances are long overdue—especially as the poor
Gentleman sitting in the urine from his pat-down ruptured colostomy bag was being
"Screened" in full view of the busy airline passenger queue. For older fliers,
Like my mother; however, who is not wheelchair-bound, walking proudly on her own
Power, TSA screening officials will have their hands full, if they even LIGHTLY
Pat her down. I would advise them to be prepared to have their surgically-gloved
Hands slapped, depending upon where they put them.

ഇരു

Out of Touch

Ah, ex-GOP Governor, Mitt Romney:
The former Governor from Massachusetts, who fashioned a mandated
Health care law, amazingly similar in size and scope to President Obama's
Mandated "Affordable Health Care" law.

Yes, ex-GOP Governor, Mitt Romney:
The smiling, perfect hair and Pepsodent white teeth GQ cover, who jokingly
Placed a $10,000 bet with Republican colleague, Rick Perry, as though that
Particular sum of money was but a trivial afterthought.

Poor ex-GOP Governor, Mitt Romney:
He certainly does not do himself any favors, with the hardworking blue collar
Crowd, not to mention the dwindling ranks of the US middle class, as he
Elaborates on buying his wife two expensive Cadillacs, or preens over paying
A lower income tax rate than most Americans on his roughly $300 million wealth.
(And then there's always that offhanded $10,000 bet thing).

Sad ex-GOP Governor, Mitt Romney:
He does not do himself any favors with Southerners, either, by casually informing
Them that he is learning to say "ya'll," or showering praise upon his ingested
Plate of grits. Please! Couldn't he have simply started one of his Southern-stump
Speeches with "How are ya'll doing, today?" instead of referencing the word
As though it was derived from some foreign language? And believe me—catering
To Southerners' stereotypically perceived culinary delights is only found insulting.

Voters in the South do not like feeling discounted by a millionaire who leaves
Them behind, without a second thought and with shoulder-shrugging ambivalence.
The rest of America does not take well to a millionaire who can drop $10,000
On a casual bet, while they struggle to pay their rent. And so—if Mr. Romney
Feels he is the "best" candidate to represent the American people, good luck at
Influencing the financially downtrodden of this, with his world of glamorous
Republican fundraisers and sparkling champagne cocktails.

Maybe, if Mr. Romney paid every single person he seeks political backing from
$10,000; he might garner the real-time political support he is so desperately seeking?

ഇരു

Detroit Tiger

On the harried US campaign trail, 2012 GOP candidate, Mitt Romney
Made a grand showcase to potential Michigan voters, where he hammered
Home his casual statement: "Let big auto fail."

He (Romney) slammed President Obama for granting the auto industry bailout,
Seeing nothing at all wrong with showering car assembly plant workers
With mountains of end-of-the-year Christmas pink slips.

And so, my advice to Mr. Romney would be: Politicians who live in anti-auto
Industry bailout glass houses should really not be expecting high pro-auto worker
Political support, now should they?

They might, more likely, expect UAW-stamped bricks to shatter the glass.

ଚ୦ଔଓ

Fondue, Anyone?

As if Syrian President (i.e. dictator) Bashar al-Assad's genocide against his
Own people was not bad enough; we now have personal e-mails exchanged
Between him and his "modern" Muslim wife, that have been leaked to the
Outraged world media community.

Does Mr. Assad convey any concern about the problems his country is
Embroiled in, via the e-mails? Not at all. Does his wife express doubts
Or indeed, even minor concerns, over the Syrian military's thug-like killing
Actions, on her husband's orders? Uh-uh.

No—our lovable (not) "Mrs." Assad, instead uses her private e-mail account,
To order expensive jewelry, along with a high-end culinary fondue set. I mean,
Who cares about Syrian citizens being gunned down by the thousands, as long as
She can still entertain guests at her exclusive dinner parties, yes?

And while the Syrian city of Homs is bombed into lifeless rubble, with its
Inhabitants' blood spattered on every street corner, Mr. Assad e-mails his wife
Lyrics from a Blake Shelton country ballad, imploring her to "stay with him,"
Until the "hard times are past." How romantic, right?

I think if the average repressed Syrian citizen were to get their hands on
Mrs. Assad's prized fondue skewers, the exclusive dinner party setting would
Come to an immediate and well-deserved end.

ᨠᨣ

Bye-Bye, Blago

Former Illinois Governor, Rod Blagojevich has begun his fourteen-year
Federal prison stint, on political corruption charges, at a Colorado penitentiary.
"Blago," as he is addressed by his nick-name, called a news conference the
Afternoon before he was to report to US Department of Correction officials,
Where he thanked all of his die-hard supporters and waved his smiling goodbyes.
One would think Mr. Blagojevich was embarking on a Caribbean resort vacation,
Rather than surrendering himself to prison authorities.

I have a distinct feeling that "Blago" will not be smiling, once the Supermax prison
Cell door slams shut behind him. And by the time he emerges back onto the political
Scene, fourteen-years later; I doubt anyone will care that he once tried to auction
Off Barack Obama's Illinois Senate seat to the highest bidder. (What? Such brazen
Political corruption, in a US state notorious for its "pay-to-play" politics?). In fact,
In an era where noteworthy political figures have a shelf-life of .001 Nano-seconds;
Mr. Blagojevich will discover that America has moved on, without his obscenity-
Laced tirades, his shady political machinations, and his over-the-top hair, which
Could give Donald Trump's rumpled coiffure a run for its money.

ಬಌಣ

The "See-Say" See-Saw

Law enforcement officials in Grapevine, Texas shot a promotional
Video for the public, highlighting their "If you see it, say something
About it" citizen watch program, where city residents were encouraged
To report suspicious activities and/or individuals in or around their
Neighborhoods to the police department.

Now—on the face of it, the program appears innocuous. Crime watch
Neighborhood patrol groups have been around for quite some time.
What is different about the "See-Say" watch group; however, is that it places
Emphasis on reporting ANY aspect in the neighborhood that even remotely
Appears out-of-place. If the UPS man has a swarthy, Middle Eastern complexion,
Call the police. If your neighbor's pesky dog is urinating on your prize rose bush,
Call the police. If a Muslim woman is spotted wearing a head scarf, call the police.
In fact, if you dislike your neighbor's front yard pink flamingo, call the police.

Grapevine law enforcement, it seems, wants to know every little (so-called)
Suspicious detail that goes on in their citizens' neighborhoods, justifying their
"See-Say" program under the guise of protecting Americans in the "War on Terror."
My question, in answer to this program is: How does spying on one's neighbors,
Then "reporting" them to the police, better their neighborhood? They are not
Deterring crime; they are simply playing adult "tattle-tales," rushing to their
Telephones to report on anyone who does not conform to "their" estimation of
Properly patriotic "War on Terror" standards and practices.

This is hardly a new concept—George W. Bush Attorney General, John Ashcroft
Introduced neighborhood spying programs, on a national US scale, via his
Dubious "Operation TIPS" program—where US businesses with access to
Americans' homes (cable TV installers, for example) were encouraged to record
Notes on anything they deemed as "suspicious" inside the dwelling. I suppose if
My cable guy had witnessed my Fahrenheit 9/11 DVD, I would have been
Visited by dour-faced FBI officials, ruminating over why a nice, clean-cut young
Woman would possess such an unpatriotic film?

In any event, there is a clear line drawn between keeping a watchful eye, as a
Deterrent against neighborhood crime, and citizens rushing to "turn in" their
(Allegedly) suspicious neighbors to police authorities, like Gestapo informants
In an old WWII Nazi movie.

৪১৫৪

Not Quite eHarmony

Recently, a CNN morning news host expounded upon what Mitt Romney's
Advertisement on an Internet "dating" site, targeting potential voters might
Look like. I would now like to present my take on what that "Personal ad"
Might encompass:

Mitt Romney, here:

"Wealthy millionaire seeks open-minded, robust voting individuals, unafraid to
Showcase their personal wealth. I am into 'changing my mind,' on issues, at a
Moment's notice; buying expensive items for friends and loved ones; and sturdy plastic
Dog crate carriers; that may be securely attached to car roofs. Voters must love dogs,
Making large cash wagers at opportunistic whims, and ignoring any/all tax return inquires."

₧₧

Stand Your Ground

Sanford, Florida neighborhood "watch captain," George Zimmerman racially-
Profiled seventeen year-old African-American, Trayvon Martin, while on security
"Patrol" of a prestigious gated community—singling him out and physically
Following him, after witnessing him merely walking past the ritzy Florida homes.

Mr. Zimmerman vociferously denies that he racially-profiled Trayvon Martin.
After following the young man in his SUV, pursuing him on foot (ignoring
Instructions from Florida police that he did "not need to do that"); he verbally
Confronted the teen with these words, clearly heard on Trayvon's cell phone:
"What are you doing here?"

Adding to Mr. Zimmerman's denial of racial profiling, is the recorded 911 cell
Phone statement he (Zimmerman) made of: "F—king coons!" Now—to me,
That appears to be rather blatantly biased, if not downright racist, from an individual
Who espouses cherished African-American family members. Is that what George
Zimmerman thinks of them, too?

After a physical confrontation with Trayvon Martin, where the young teen's
Desperate voice is heard screaming for help, a single gunshot from Mr. Zimmerman's
Nine millimeter handgun rings out into the night. The heartsick cries for help
Immediately cease, after the shot, casting doubt upon Zimmerman's claim that HE
Is the one crying out for assistance.

Then, with Trayvon lying dead, face-down in the grass of a neighborhood lawn,
Shocked witnesses exit their homes, to find Zimmerman straddling the teen's body,
With his feet to either side of his supine torso, his hands pressed violently against
His back. When asked THREE TIMES about what had transpired, or if 'everything
Was alright?', Zimmerman casually responded for them to "call the police."

Mr. Zimmerman has claimed the right of "self-defense," against Trayvon Martin,
The young African-American teenager, walking back to his father's fiancées'
Apartment complex, with a can of ice tea and a bag of Skittles in his hands. Wow—that
Certainly spells an imminent threat, if ever I heard one, right? (NOT). Utilizing Florida's
Dubious "Stand your ground" law, Zimmerman opines his brutal shooting of Trayvon
Martin was "justified," by his position as the neighborhood watch captain.

George Zimmerman is nothing more than a racial profiling thug, with neither the
Common sense to avoid a completely non-threatening life situation; but the gall to
Purport his killing actions were "justified," against a young teen, he, himself, addressed
As an "F—king coon!" And no matter how many pristine "gated community" residents
Come forward, to attest to Zimmerman's (alleged) integrity, their shallow praise rings
Hollow and untrue.

To alter a famous advertising tag-line, for a prominent insurance company:

"Like a good neighbor, the watch captain is there"—armed with an automatic weapon
And ready to shoot-to-kill, apparently.

ഇൻ

Have ID, Will Travel

The GOP has been vociferously championing multi-US state "voter ID" Laws. For those of you who might not be familiar with what "voter ID" laws Encompass—it is the practice of requiring prospective voters to show a "Legitimate" photo identification card, before they are allowed to cast their Ballot at their designated polling places.

What the GOP fails to make people aware of; however, is that the primary Focus of dubious "Voter ID" laws IS to disenfranchise voters who are not Likely to vote for Republican Party candidates (i.e. the poor or members Of the minority community). In case the GOP has forgotten, voting in US Elections is a US Constitutional "right"; it is not a voter ID-granted "privilege."

Most US states that pass voter ID laws require a notarized legal birth certificate (Not a copy), to acquire a "suitable" photo ID that will be accepted at The voting booth. In addition, the photo IDs range in price from $40 to $50 dollars. The point being, the working poor can barely afford to pay for food or rent, let alone, An extra $40 for a voter ID—or the $150-$300 fee for the notarized birth certificate Required, prior to the actual Voter ID purchase.

"We can solve that conundrum," the GOP smugly maintains. "We will provide Voter IDs, free-of-charge, to any person who wants one." I find the GOP's boast Uniquely compelling. I mean, why would the same voters, who find their polling Place voting machines mysteriously "out-of-service" on Election Day, trust that They would be able to acquire an "authorized" voter ID card in any timely fashion?

And so, as to "free" photo ID cards being provided to poverty-stricken or Minority voters; I have yet to see a US state pass a "Voter ID" law that allows for This "magnanimous" gesture, on behalf of the Republican Party. In fact, my Questions in all of this are these: Are people who do not have a proper "Voter ID" To be hauled away from their polling places by state police storm troopers?

Are poor or minority voters to be deliberately discounted, due to their being DFL supporters? And most importantly—if I am required to present a photo ID, To be able to vote; what else will I be required to present a photo ID for? To walk Around my own neighborhood? To rake leaves or pull weeds out in my front yard? Perhaps, to attend a MN public event or to be admitted to a MN amusement park?

To alter a famous advertising tag-line from a prominent US Dairy Industry television commercial for milk:

"Voter IDs—it does the Republican Party good."

༄༅

Benghazi, Libya Aftermath – A Haiku for You

Barack Obama,
On four dead Americans:
"A bump in the road."

୭୦୪

Face-Down

Inside a suburban airport, Oklahoma State Police were videotaped dragging
A handcuffed man by his ankles, with his face pressed across the airport's
Tiled flooring, as they (presumably) took him into custody.

What was the man's offense? He had merely arrived at the airport ahead
Of a campaign stop by Newt Gingrich. The man had simply wanted to ask
Mr. Gingrich some political questions.

Maybe the Oklahoma State Police thought the man's political questions
Might be incendiary or otherwise embarrassing for Mr. Gingrich? Or perhaps
The officers believed the unarmed man was (for whatever reason) dangerous?
The officers may even have been Gingrich supporters, who did not want to see
"Their" guy verbally put on-the-spot?

In any case, dragging ANY individual, with their arms handcuffed behind
Their back and their face planted across the cold floor conjures up images of
Nazi storm troopers dragging their luckless victims into Gestapo torture cells.
It is a highly-unflattering portrait to both Oklahoma, as well as to the state's
Entire police force.

My advice to the Oklahoma State Police would be to treat people with the
Same common courtesy and respect with which they expect (if not demand)
To be accorded, themselves.

When and if it does become wrong, to question our political officials;
We will have reverted to a totalitarian police state Vladimir Putin or upstart
North Korean successor, Kim Jung Un, would be proud of.

Cinemascope with Stereophonic Sound

On the 2012 General Election campaign trail, the US public was treated to orchestrated Film "events," anywhere from five to thirty minutes long, where political candidates Vying for the US Presidency either soulfully expounded upon their own virtues or Verbally berated their opponents.

Cases in point:

We first had morally-challenged Newt Gingrich, whose ultra-rich Super PAC funded a Half-hour film "documentary" against GOP rival, Mitt Romney. The video, entitled: "When Mitt Romney Came to Town" did nothing, save heralding Romney's dismal Record, as the CEO of Bain Capital, where pink slips were handed out by the gross To US companies deemed unprofitable by the venture capitalist group, and only a Strategic "handful" of workplaces were saved, by Bain's calculated "angel investing."

Next, we had US President Barack Obama, whose re-election team pieced together A seventeen-minute video montage, entitled: "The Road We've Travelled." The Entire clip highlights Mr. Obama's alleged political achievements, with the resounding Look and feel of the African-American US Civil Rights movement. No mention was Made, as to how Mr. Obama intended to better the foundering US economy; only how "His" policies, enacted while President, were all idyllic and wonderful.

And lastly, we had Rick Santorum jumping into the propaganda fray, with a slickly Designed and produced video segment, charmingly titled: "Obamaville."
The entire piece (part of a film "series," I am told) did absolutely NOTHING to suggest How a Rick Santorum presidency would have brought America back from the (alleged) Brink of destruction—instead, it painted a profound portrait of apocalyptic doom, Wrought on the US in 2014, two years after President Obama was re-elected.

If I might address each of these film biopics:

Newt Gingrich's movie-of-the-week simply demonstrated how much wealth his Super PAC Investors (I mean supporters) held, and how they would stop at no lengths, to Denigrate any political candidate deemed as a credible threat to "their" man.

President Obama's video piece presented nothing more than hopelessly positive, spin-Induced administration hype—and not entirely factually supported hype, at that.

And all Rick Santorum's segment of video sludge managed to do, was to blatantly
Showcase how vindictive and utterly repugnant he (Santorum) was, toward not only
ANY US President, who happened to be a Democrat—but especially toward an
African-American President Santorum vilified as a (allegedly) "Muslim-Socialist,
Determined to wreak class warfare and to redistribute all of America's wealth."

Please! If I want to watch a film that actually satisfies; I'll pop open my DVD player
And insert a copy of the Disney-Pixar animated movie, "Up."

ℴℴ

House of Cards

Whenever any potential detractor criticizes US President Barack Obama,
No matter what the political subject might be, his administration is very
Quick to point to them, as being racially-biased. This is called playing the
"Race card," for those of you who might not be aware of it.

Now—President Obama does have his legitimate share of racially-biased, if
Not downright racist detractors, most notably represented by the vindictive
Tea Party crowd. However, to blatantly paint any and all individuals, who
Dare to question the President with the (allegedly) anti-African-American
"Race card" dynamic is only found insulting.

If any individual does not care for Mr. Obama's political platforms, and presents
An intelligent, composed, factually-based argument to support their position; they
Are not automatically voicing their concern(s), because he is African-American.
Some are speaking their political minds, which happen to not be in agreement with
Him. Like it or not, not everyone who expresses their displeasure with President
Obama is anti-African-American; or indeed, anti-minority, whatsoever.

I would like to point out that the proverbial "race card" plays both ways.

In the 2008 US general election, members of the "New Black Panthers" stood
Outside of select polling places, dressed in armed military regalia, to intimidate
Voters into voting for Mr. Obama. (The new "Panthers" are a loosely-based
Derivative of the old 1960's and 1970's counter-culture group—who adamantly
Disassociate themselves with them, I might add).

The point being, both sides play the "race card," whenever it suits them to do so;
Whether it is irate white people blaming African-Americans for their neighborhood's
Heightening crime rate; or African-Americans angrily vilifying current-day
Caucasians, whom they still hold directly responsible for Sixteenth and Seventeenth
Century slavery practices.

Sigh—can't we all just get along and respect one another as equals, without
Automatically pouncing upon any perceived disagreement as being somehow
Derived from or motivated by race?

ಬೆಂ

Have a Heart

Former George W. Bush Vice President and unapologetic supporter of torture,
Dick Cheney recently received an anonymous donor heart, in a sweeping
Organ transplant operation, at the ripe old age of 71.

Never mind those individuals, who may have been waiting for the same heart,
For a longer timeframe than twenty months; or were in greater (not to mention
Younger) need of it—good old Dick's lifetime elected office health insurance
Forks over the cash (on the US taxpayers' dime) and the demonically grinning
Figure, celebrated as the evil "Darth Vader," is awarded the heart.

I hear poor Mr. Cheney will have to take daily medication(s), to prevent his
Body from rejecting his new heart. I suppose when the body is accustomed to
Accommodating a cold heart carved out of stone, it makes accepting a warm
Donor heart a difficult hurdle to overcome.

Say—why doesn't Dick give his "new" heart a torture workout? I mean,
Simulated drowning (i.e. waterboarding) can really do wonders for testing those
Cardiac boundaries, right?

⁎⁎⁎

Let's Not Forget About George W. Bush (A Haiku for You)

Sad George W:
He wrecked the economy,
Grinned, and left office.

ഇൻ

Your Password, Please

A great many prospective employers have resorted to the pre-employment
Interview policy of requiring work applicants to supply them with the
Passwords to their Facebook social media pages.

I am a bit confused, as to ANY company's legal right to require confidential
Social media passwords; however, employment lawyers assure me that the
Sordid practice is completely within nosy employers' rights.

And this course of action is not reserved for pre-employment—not at all.
In fact, if the employer decides, for ANY reason, that they wish to access their
Employees' Facebook pages, they simply demand the password required to do so.

I applaud a recent job interviewee, who—after being prodded for their Facebook
Password—politely declined, disgustedly remarking that: "They would not want
To work for an employer who would stoop to demanding confidential information."

Now—I suspect the person interviewing for the job in question had nothing to
Hide on their Facebook page. Having a workplace require one's confidential
Information, as a pre-cursor to employment; however, hearkens back to the days
Of proving one's "innocence" before the Spanish Inquisition.

Private social media passwords are exactly that—private. And if potential
Employers want to cultivate trusting, loyal employees; they might want to start by
Leaving confidential materials they have no respectful right to obtain out of the
Pre-employment equation or the company-centric dogma.

☜☞

Revelations

Trayvon Martin's (the African-American teen shot dead by dubious
Neighborhood watch "captain," George Zimmerman) reputation is now being
Assailed by various Sanford, Florida officials, who seemingly will stop at
Nothing to paint the slain young man as a shifty juvenile delinquent.

Beginning with his confidential school records being released to the media;
Detailing Trayvon's suspension for having a plastic baggie inside his
Backpack containing marijuana residue, to the original Florida State Attorney,
Norm Wolfinger vehemently denying HE denied a Sanford Police Detective's
Request to arrest George Zimmerman, on the night of Travyon's killing; the
Sanford City Hall has labored to make "their" actions appear good, at the expense
Of making a dead African-American teen look bad.

Even if Trayvon Martin was suspended for (allegedly) being in the possession of
Marijuana (actually, the baggie found inside his backpack was empty, containing
Drug residue, only, NOT the drug, itself); what difference does this make, to the
Ongoing investigation into his killing—other than to specifically discredit a young
Man, who aspired to be a commercial airline pilot's reputation?

I know this might come as something of a (gasp!) surprise to Sanford, Florida
Officials; but most teens have engaged in poor decision making or been complicit
In school troublemaking episodes. Does the Sanford City Hall's allegations, indicate
That George Zimmerman was "justified," in his racially profiling actions, leaving
Trayvon Martin dead, face-down across a perfectly landscaped, rain-soaked lawn?

No—George Zimmerman is NOT the gated community "hero," protecting its poor,
Pitiful wealthy Florida residents against some unknown African-American male,
Who (supposedly) had no right to be present in their neighborhood. Mr. Zimmerman
Is the racially-biased aggressor, showcasing his African-American scorn, on recorded
911 calls, indicating Trayvon Martin was "suspicious," due to his being black.

And despite what Mr. Zimmerman maintains; Florida's "Stand Your Ground" law
Does NOT protect him, as the primary aggressor in an entirely avoidable confrontation.
As to a Zimmerman family member's assertion that George Zimmerman was on his way
To a local Target—and not even "neighborhood watch captaining," at all, I wonder how
Many people peruse their Target stores with loaded nine millimeter handguns hidden
Inside their waistline firearm holsters? (Outside of Texas, that is).

൫൦

Round Two

Wisconsin Governor, Scott Walker, who made it his single-minded
Obsession to rid his state of any/all union collective bargaining rights,
Found himself the despised target of a state "recall" election.

After deriding his detractors, passing them off as "unorganized,
Non-pivotal cogs in the liberal machine," he was surprised (or was it
Astounded) to survey the results of the widely-circulated "recall" petition.
(The petition needed 900,000 certified signatures, in order for the
"Recall" election to proceed—it garnered over two million).

Sadly, Scott Walker retained his gubernatorial seat; although not by as
Wide a voting margin as his campaign headquarters purported. I'm sure
He celebrated his win with high-end champagne, when informed that his
Draconian method of "governing" Wisconsin had triumphed.

"Governor" Walker might like to keep this principle in mind, before once again
Assuming Gubernatorial power with the malevolent aplomb of a "my way or the
Highway" figure: "A little (collective) bargaining—i.e. compromise—goes a long way."

As the youth of several generations past once remarked:
"See you in the funny papers, 'Governor' Walker."

ଚଠଓଷ

Street Cred

Much ado has been made about Republican Mitt Romney's dubious "big name" GOP political endorsements. If I might address each of these (supposedly) pivotal endorsements, I would like to point out some rather unsavory aspects to them.

The endorsement from former US President George H.W. Bush:

An out-of-touch, wealthy elitist who was drummed out of the US White
House, for being an out-of-touch, wealthy elitist does not carry a whole
Lot of political weight, except within the die-hard Republican ranks.
And poor Mr. Romney really does not need the support of one out-of-touch,
Wealthy elitist hand washing the other, now does he? Especially, when he,
Himself, is viewed as being an out-of-touch, wealthy elitist?

The endorsement from freshman Florida Tea Party Senator, Marco Rubio:

An "endorsement" that rings with all of the hollow clarity of someone who
Has reluctantly resigned themselves to the inescapable fate of HAVING to
Support Romney, because he is a fellow-Republican. There was nothing about the
Alleged "Go Mitt!" applause from Mr. Rubio that even remotely rang genuine.
Here's a hint, Marco—at least SMILE, when you throw your support behind your
Fellow GOP colleague, huh? (That and don't drink bottled water when delivering
Televised party rebuttals).

The endorsement from former US President, George W. Bush:
A chagrined endorsement equated to the political "kiss-of-death." (Along with
Donald Trump).

And so—as for Mitt Romney's (alleged) "big name" GOP endorsements;
I wouldn't be too proud or smugly grinning at having them, when taking into account
Their less-than-admirable, seamy political undersides.

∞ℂℤ

Not Suitable for Prime Time

Ensconced in the final throes of his rubber stamp Russian Presidency,
Dmitry Medvedev met with US President, Barack Obama at a South Korean
Summit, where the two world leaders discussed (among other things),
America's military commitment to its NATO allies, in the form of a
Defensive "missile shield," protecting them against incoming bombardment.

Leaning forward, as though he and President Medvedev were sharing
A special secret, President Obama spoke these words, under his breath,
Which happened to be picked up by a live news media outlet microphone:
"This is my last election. After my election, I have more flexibility."
It is important to note that President Obama's remarks were totally candid,
Spoken within the context that he did NOT know they were being recorded.

President Medvedev nodded, informally, (apparently, also unaware that he
Was speaking to a "live" media audience), replying: "I'll make sure that
Vladimir (i.e. incoming Russian President, Vladimir Putin) is aware of that."
Both world leaders then smiled, as though the two of them had uttered some
Immensely clever verbal commentary.

I don't know which aspect of this off-the-cuff verbal exchange I find to be the
Most disturbing—that the US needs to grovel before a nefarious Russian thug,
Bargaining for the "flexible" right to protect our NATO allies? That the US even
Desires "flexibility" with a country who so "flexibly" supports Bashar al-Assad's
Brutal Syrian crackdown, along with a "flexible" nuclear Iran? Or perhaps the
"Flexible" arrogance of President Obama, at simply assuming "he" would be the
De-facto re-elected US President, in a US general election outcome?

Note for future reference: Whispered conversations a US President does not want
The public to be privy to are best conducted within the bowels of the Central
Intelligence Agency or in ex-VP, Dick Cheney's infamous underground bunker.

෨෬

Sour Grapes

On the heels of his being disagreeable, at having a private conversation with
Outgoing Russian President, Dmitry Medvedev recorded, via a live news media
Outlet; President Barack Obama harbored clear indignation with the
Conservative majority of the US Supreme Court, as they deliberated the various
Legal tenets of his (Mr. Obama's) mandated "Affordable Health Care" law.

President Obama voiced his complaints against the high court's numerous
Inquiries into the health care legislation (affecting the health insurance outcomes
Of all Americans) with the facial expression and voice tone of a toddler being
Told "no" by its parents.

The President verbally berated the Supreme Court for engaging in "judicial activism,"
Whining that the high court is not an elected, but an "appointed" governing body.
The concept of an appointed US Supreme Court, holding judicial power for life, is set
Down within the US Constitution; and I certainly did not hear Mr. Obama complaining,
When he propelled his two chosen nominees into its lifetime ranks. The neo-con 5-4
Majority is the primary point of contention—inside or outside of the US White House.

It should be noted that the problems attributed to this majority are nothing new.
THIS majority brought us the principle of US corporations being able to legally "buy"
elections;
They allowed for police officers to kick in anyone's door, if they "smelled" (alleged)
Marijuana; and let's not forget their most infamous 5-4 majority decision—where
George W. Bush was "appointed" the 2000 US President, after the last Florida voter
Recount (showing Al Gore in the lead) was arbitrarily halted.

President Obama is hardly the first individual to be highly disappointed by the US high
Court. And yes, the Supreme Court DOES engage in "judicial activism," no matter
How vehemently they deny that fact. I hear they have ruled that ANY police officer
May strip-search ANY arrested individual, for ANY law infraction. What with neo-con
Justice Scalia's affinity for orgies, and neo-con Justice Thomas' lurid sexual harassment
background; is anyone really surprised?

In June of 2012, the High Court ruled that the President's "Affordable Health Care"
Law WAS Constitutional; however, the "penalties" the Obama Administration utilized,
For those who did not secure health insurance via its official "mandate" were, instead,
Classified as a "tax," as opposed to a "fee."

So much for the President's boast that he would not raise taxes on anyone other than
America's wealthiest citizens.

⁂⁜

(Roving) Eye of Newt

Ah, Newt Gingrich—that alleged everyman, who cheated on
His first two wives, while they were hospitalized; sallying forth,
To marry his third voluptuous blonde bedroom conquest.

Yes, Newt Gingrich—that alleged "family values" supporter,
Who remarked that his first sick wife was not "young enough or
Pretty enough to be the (US) President's wife."

My, Newt Gingrich—that realistic pinnacle of chauvinism,
Self-righteously imagining a working scenario, where he would
Even be elected to the US Presidency, in the first place.

Watch out, current "Mrs." Calista Gingrich:
You've won yourself the equivalent of the garish stuffed animal
Nobody wants from the gambling midway at a State Fair.

৪৩

Candy Slogans

Ah, that colorful Texas Governor, Rick Perry:

He, who is so enamored of invoking his state's unique succession clause,
Threatening to secede from the Union, whenever he becomes outraged,
Or throws a childish political tantrum.

A prestigious candy company had a hit advertising slogan for two
Of their select candy bars, which I think summarizes Mr. Perry quite well:
"Sometimes you feel like a nut" (Texas); "Sometimes you don't" (Rest of the US).

ജന്‍ജ

Fix It

"Do you have a problem with your son or daughter being gay?
Have they come out of the closet, at the most importune time?
Have no fear! Just send them to my husband's and my
'Christian' counseling services clinic. We'll take the time to
Talk with them and to convince them that they are living a deviant
Lifestyle. If that doesn't work, we'll belittle them into believing
They are abnormal and deserving of our derision.
'We' will pray over their homosexual or lesbian tendencies;
Mixing 'our' spirituality with unfounded psychological practice."

"Yes, friends, neighbors, colleagues, and constituents:
If your children are broken by the disease of homosexuality,
Send them to us and we'll lovingly coerce them to embrace a
A 'can-do' spirit of heterosexual change.
It's not too late to bully them into a sexual orientation meltdown;
And if they refuse to listen; we will gladly throw them into the street:
We don't 'force' any lewd gay person to accept our program to recovery.
Oh and don't worry about that pesky 'reparative therapy' moniker,
It's completely untrue. We 'fix'; we don't 'repair'."

[I'm Michele Bachmann and I approved this message.]

৪০৪৪

No Thanks

Former US President George W. Bush turned down an invite
From US President Barak Obama, when Mr. Obama convened
A commemorative ceremony for 9/11 victims at Ground Zero
In Manhattan. The ceremony was to celebrate the assassination
Of 9/11's mastermind and Al-Qaeda founding father,
Osama Bin Laden.

I am assuming Mr. Bush did not care to attend, for several
Mitigating reasons, among which included he promised the
American people that finding Bin Laden was his administration's
Greatest priority; then scarcely six months later, informed them
That he did not know where Bin Laden was, nor did he care.

And then there is always the factor of his (Bush's) not having
Been able to find or neutralize Bin Laden, throughout the entire
Eight year tenure of his Presidency. Also, as a faux "Texan,"
(Birthplace: Connecticut), Mr. Bush was probably miffed that
A "person of color" was able to accomplish something that a
"Good old boy" (Redneck-speak) was not.

In any event, George W's turning down the opportunity
To honor 9/11 victims and to celebrate the demise of the man
Who orchestrated the 9/11 attacks speaks far more loudly
Than any stirring speech he delivered with his bullhorn,
Standing atop smoldering Ground Zero rubble.

ಬಂಚ

Sound Byte

Minnesota Republican US Congresswoman, Michele Bachmann,
Remarks to any outstretched media or podium microphone,
That the first thing her GOP colleagues need to do, is to "repeal Obamacare."
Pundits ask her any question about any of her political platforms;
And her response is: "We need to repeal Obamacare.

How does Congress plan to get the nation's tumultuous deficit under control?
Bachmann: "We need to repeal Obamacare."
How does Congress plan to handle the War in Afghanistan?
Bachmann: "We need to repeal Obamacare."

How does Congress propose to deal with global warming?
Bachmann: "We need to repeal Obamacare—besides, global warming is a hoax."
How can Congress strengthen America's National Security?
Bachmann: "We need to repeal Obamacare."

How should Congress handle intricacies in the "War on Terror?"
Bachmann: "We need to repeal Obamacare."
How will Congress help decrease the US' staggering unemployment rate?
Bachmann: "We need to repeal Obamacare."

The response has become so immediately customary, that I can
Only imagine if one of her cherubic foster children asked her for
A glass of orange juice, Ms. Bachmann's response would be:
"I'll get it for you, as soon as we repeal Obamacare."

෨෮

Not Quite the Flintstones

In honor of everything having to do with our fumbling friends at the
Federal Emergency Management Agency (FEMA), I would like to present
A memorable TV cartoon sing-song within a new light:

FEMA! Meet the FEMA!
They're a large disaster family;

From the town of D.C.,
They're a sad page out of history,

Someday, maybe they will get things right,
Then they'll be able to fix a plight.

When you're with the FEMA,
It's a Yabba-dabba-do time,

Hard to find food time;
We'll have a dismal time!

[Insert cherry, twelve second big band musical interlude]

Repeat: We'll have a dismal time!
(Screaming): FEMA!

 –

ജ

Can't Happen Here

We don't need to worry about our country's aging nuclear plants;
Those close-minded naysayers are always touting what might
Possibly happen, should any of them have a major problem.
A Japanese Fukushima Daiichi nuclear plant malfunction could
Never happen here—America is not prone to tsunamis generated
By category nine and above earthquakes, except in California,
And then all of our nuclear plants are far enough inland to be safe.
Why, none of our nuclear plants has ever experienced a measurable
Radiation leak or any semblance of a dreaded "China Syndrome."

If I were to answer these ludicrous safety boasts; I might point out
That their "facts" did not include a palpable radiation contamination
At Florida's Turkey Creek Nuclear Plant during Hurricane Andrew,
Or the memorably famous near-China syndrome experienced at
Pennsylvania's Three Mile Island Nuclear Plant. Never mind the fact
That these aging plants are only sporadically checked by the US Nuclear
Regulatory Commission (NRC), not to mention their "security"
Against a prospective terrorist attack is often a non-existent joke.

So much for the "It can't happen here" mentality. It has already happened;
It was simply not available to a media sluggish, pre-Internet/Facebook/
Twitter landscape—where the US Government and senior nuclear industry
Officials still controlled every piece of information released to the public.

ꙮꙨꙮ

Lockstep

"USA...USA...USA." When I hear that chant uttered mindlessly,
As an unspoken gage of an individual's acceptable "patriotism";
Or as a backdrop to George W. Bush defending his horrendous
Human rights record, while simultaneously justifying his administration's
Lackadaisical use of torture; or as the measure of how truly "American"
A person is—I envision a singular quotation from Ralph Waldo Emerson:

"When a whole nation is roaring patriotism at the top of its voice;
I am fain to explore the cleanness of its hands and purity of its heart."

Chant "USA" to show you are truly patriotic; not because you have
Ingested alcohol at a NASCAR event; or feel yourself superior to others;
Or are marching in a lockstep conga line, engineered by the
US Department of Homeland Security as an (alleged) show of support for
"National Security." Your country's name is far too precious, to become
A commonplace, haughty euphemism.

☙❧

To Protect and Serve

In Rochester, New York, a woman relaxing after work in her pajamas
Witnessed Rochester Police pull over a vehicle—practically in front
Of her house, on a public neighborhood street. When the "pull-over"
Appeared to be turning heavy-handed, the woman grasped her
Cell phone and began videotaping the event.

When the officers realized the woman was recording their actions
On-camera, one of Rochester's finest remarked that she was causing him
To feel "uneasy." There was no command to "back up"; no order to "cease
And desist" from her actions—just a casual observation that the officer
Felt uneasy. Felt uneasy with what, I might inquire?

Was the officer concerned at being in an unknown neighborhood,
At night? Was he disturbed at feeling someone's (legal) presence from
Over his shoulder? Did he feel the woman was actively threatening him?
Or was he simply upset that the opportunity to use his night stick was
Being recorded for all posterity?

Despite being issued no directive to stop her taping, the woman was
Eventually knocked to the ground and arrested, and her cell phone
Confiscated. When officials higher within the Rochester chain of
Police command came to their senses; the woman was released
Without charge—although I am unsure as to the fate of her cell phone?

I have great respect for law enforcement; however, it is instances such
As these, which serve to perpetuate the (often very real) stereotype
Of police brutality or of playing the unquestioned dictator, due to standing
Behind a badge. I can only wonder, in horror, what the officers in the Rodney
King beating would have done, had they realized they were being recorded?

And so, if this "right to privacy" disgrace ever made its way to the Supreme Court?

The US Supreme Court recently ruled that law enforcement officers could kick
In the door of anyone, should they smell any even minor semblance of marijuana.
I highly doubt they would lose any sleep over officers' mandating what ordinary,
Law-abiding citizens may or may not videotape, while standing in the (supposed)
Legality and safety of their front yard.

80CB

Red Flag

I remember actually shuddering, as I slid the DVD on the
Weather Underground from its public library shelf:
I mean, with the FBI monitoring everybody's library check outs,
What might they think of my viewing a documentary on a known
Domestic terrorist group? Would they think I was in cahoots
With the 1970's-era revolutionaries; or would they assume my
Association with the DVD meant that I viewed the US Government
With distrustful suspicion? If I viewed the US Government with
Distrustful suspicion, what might that predispose me to do—construct
A pipe bomb in my kitchen or throw a grenade at the Pentagon?

With my heart pounding and my palms sweating, I carried the DVD
To the library check-out station. The second I scanned the film's
Barcode, I had visions of FBI officials swooping out from hidden
Nooks and crannies, to cart me off to prison—or at least to an
Underground interrogation cell, where they could better ascertain
Why a nice, clean-cut young Caucasian woman would want to
Check out a documentary on a known domestic terrorist group?
No one confronted me at the checkout station; however, I felt unseen
Eyes following me the entire walking distance from the library
To my car parked outside.

It is a sad state of affairs, when ordinary citizens and library patrons
Are forced to nervously consider what materials they choose to read
And/or watch, as they safeguard themselves against FBI suspicion(s).
I made it to my living space, without being pulled over by black SUVs,
With heavily-tinted windows, and no one arrived at my door, to question
My documentary motives; but I did hear ominous "clicking" noises over
My land line telephone receiver.

80C3

Famine is in the Eye of the Beholder

We at the GOP can be persuaded by the United Nations'
Designation of a disastrous famine occurring in the lawless
African nation of Somalia. We are not completely heartless;
No matter what our scowling Democratic opponents insist.

We at the GOP are not opposed to sending massive food
Airlifts or UN food supplies to the lawless African nation
Of Somalia—even in spite of its elitist class of pirates, who
Systematically attack and raid all ships off of their coastline.

We at the GOP would be willing to distribute life-saving
Food aid to the hordes of starving people in the lawless
African nation of Somalia—wait a minute—what's that?
The food would be distributed by the terrorist group, Al-Shabbab?

Forget everything we just announced or were predisposed
To help with—we cannot support any terrorist organization,
Especially an organization with such close ties to Al-Qaeda;
Those who are starving will simply have to continue to starve.

And don't blame us, for not lifting a finger to help the lawless
African nation of Somalia's famine plight. It is Al-Shabab's
Fault. As long as they continue to strive against American interests;
Their fellow countrymen will continue to suffer the starvation consequences.

Now remember, disgruntled people of Somalia—it is Al-Shabab's
Fault that you are hungry; deal with them, once and for all, and UN bags
Of rice will parachute down from above, while food supplies will be
Happily passed out by UN peacekeeping motorcades.

ഇ൦ഌ

Showdown in Hobbit Land

Arizona Republican Senator, John McCain read from a
Wall Street Journal editorial on the US Senate floor, comparing
The Tea Party to "hobbits" from the pages of J.R.R. Tolkien's
"Lord of the Rings" literary fantasy. Mr. McCain offered no verbal
Support of the WSJ editorial—but simply read how a well-known
And respected US newspaper views meddling and accusatorily
Disruptive Tea Party political elements.

Tea Party favorite, Sharon Angle—you remember her, right?
She was unceremoniously defeated in the US 2010 midterm
Election against Nevada DFL stalwart, Harry Reid. Ms. Angle
Immediately accused John McCain of "name calling" and issued a
Childish retort worthy of any decent Kindergarten tantrum:
"In the (Lord of the Rings) books; the hobbits are the heroes and
Save the land." How nice of Ms. Angle to point this critical detail
Out to the science fiction & fantasy reading bereft public.

I am not entirely certain how merely reading an editorial from a
Newspaper equates to Mr. McCain's "name calling" of the Tea Party;
If anything, the WSJ columnist was the one doing the "name calling."
Ms. Angle does have a vicious temper, regarding her beloved teapots, though.
I suppose, considering her open approach to "solve election results
You don't like" with "Second Amendment" right-to-bear-arms solutions;
We are probably fortunate she did not draw a nine millimeter handgun and
Shoot Senator McCain in the head.

ഇഇ

Broken Record

On the heels of a police officer in Rochester, New York knocking a woman
To the ground and placing her under arrest, for simply videotaping a traffic
Stop he was involved in on a public street in front of her house; we now have
An Ohio police officer placed on administrative leave, following two instances,
Where he verbally threatened the individuals he had pulled over.

Now, some people might think that a police officer verbally berating someone
They have pulled over during a traffic stop is not anything to become upset over.
I, however, happen to disagree. There is no call for police officers, who should
Be held to a higher standard than non-law enforcement citizens, to blatantly
Use their authority to deliberately denigrate anyone.

If the officer encounters verbal abuse from a potential offender, during a
"Pull-over," they do not have to respond in a verbally abusive pattern.
The "pattern" of the Ohio police officer in question shows two traffic stops,
Recorded in detail by his squad car's dashboard safety camera. During one
Action, he tersely ordered an African-American male to: "Get out of your car,
Right now, or I'll shoot you in the head!" (Note: This was a suspected DUI
Stop, so the individual in question might not have been particularly alert to the
Officer's original command to exit the vehicle).

During a second exchange—incidentally, also involving a traffic stop with an
African-American male—the same officer brusquely growled: "I'm going to
Kill every last one of you!" I am a bit confused? What does the officer mean,
By the phraseology "every last one of"? Does he mean he will kill every last
Person he pulls over for a traffic stop? Does he mean he will kill every single
Individual who commits a moving violation? Or does he really mean that
He would long to kill every single African-American he comes into contact
With? With a track record as anger-challenged as his; one can hardly
Decipher who the officer in question wishes to "kill" at murderous random.

This is hardly a portrait fitting or worthy of genuine, unbiased police conduct.
I submit that this officer's unsavory commentary not only dishonors his entire
Department; but it further substantiates the widely held stereotype of police
Brutality, intimidation, and omnipotence, simply due to standing behind a
Shiny, authoritative badge.

8OC8

Boom Revisited

There's a flash of bright light and my world is turned upside down,
With my body laid flat across the metal roof to my charred Humvee:
My vision drifts in and out; I can't make out the words of anybody
Speaking around me—they sound as if they are talking in incredibly
Slow motion.

There's a rush of hot air and sand as my body is lifted out of the
Humvee's twisted wreckage. "I can't feel my legs," I think, as the
Medics check me over and attach I.V. lines to both of my arms.
"Wait a minute," I then check myself. "I can't even see my legs,"
I then ponder, confused.

There's a rush of fevered excitement in the nearby combat hospital;
Everyone is smiling down at me, assuring me that "everything is
Going to be alright." I believe them because I want to believe them.
If I don't, it means I might not be alright. Someone sinks a needle
Into one of my I.V. lines and I begin to feel warm and woozy.

There's a hush of low voices, as I emerge from being unconscious;
A pony tailed nurse with a kind smile asks me how I am feeling.
I tell her "I can't feel my legs"; and her smile becomes replaced by a
Worried facial expression. She does not have to say anything;
I know My legs are gone.

There's a flash of bright lights, as I roll down the ramp to the US
Military hospital, where intrigued media outlets are eager to capture
Images of me as a "wounded warrior" hero. I don't mind it, as long as
I get to reunite with my girl. There she is—still as beautiful as ever.
She rushes forward, grabbing me in her loving arms.

There's the feel of her cool tears across my face as she unsuccessfully
Tries to brush them out of her shining blue eyes. She says they are
From happiness to see me; not from observing me in a wheelchair
With no legs. I tell her it won't be long until I am up and walking
Again with my newly-fashioned prosthetic limbs.

There's a feeling of serenity that washes over me, as she tells me she
Loves me, with or without legs—and that she will love me forever.
When she places the baby girl I have seen but never yet held in my arms;
I am awash in a golden cocoon of peace. The media crowd is still
Snapping photographs; but my world has only three people in it.

୫୦୯୫

Smarter than You Think

"Hi—my name is Jake; and I am the family dog.
I'm a handsome German Shepherd, if I do say so, myself.
My mistress is home from Afghanistan; this time, it's for
Good, since she is missing an arm and a leg from her
Re-fueling convoy encountering an IED."

"It's OK if my mistress cannot pet me with her right hand
Anymore; the left hand will do just fine. And as soon
As her new prostheses are ready and she finishes her
Physical therapy; we'll be able to go out jogging again.
I can't wait for her to throw the Frisbee for me."

"My mistress has a lot of what humans call 'heart';
Of course, I knew that all along—she's a scrappy little
Fighter who does not take any crap from anyone. I like
That aspect about her; it reminds me of me. If anyone
Breaks into my house; be prepared to get mauled, big-time."

"Gotta' go—here comes my mistress from her PT session;
I need to rush over so she can stroke my head and coat.
Her voice is soothing as she calls me a 'good dog' and a
'Smart boy'." I lap it up, fawning over her with an endless
Barrage of wet kisses."

"Bye, now—my name is Jake and I am the family dog.
I'm on the move, accompanying my mistress as the orderly
Pushes her wheelchair over to the US veterans' shuttle.
It's been nice talking with you."

[This poem and its immediate predecessor were written in honor of
All Iraq and Afghanistan US military veterans who have lost limbs in the
Service of their country.]

෨෬

Blame Game

As to the downgrade of the US' credit rating from AAA to AA+ by
Standard and Poor's (S & P); here are the primary responses assigning blame
For the creditworthiness diminution:

From the Democrats:
"There, you see! Our Republican colleagues' constant bickering over whether or
Not they can appease their meddlesome Tea Party fold over no tax increases and
No restrictions on corporate tax loopholes is what brought us to S & P's lowering
Of America's credit rating! Why can't they get their polarized act together and
Subscribe to partisan efforts to confront debt ceiling crises?"

From the Republicans:
"There, you see! Our Democratic colleagues' constant bickering over whether
Or not they can avoid angering their welfare state voter base over cutting into
The entitlement programs that are bleeding America's financial reserves dry
Is what brought us to S & P's lowering of America's credit rating! Why can't
They get their polarized act together and subscribe to partisan efforts to confront
Debt ceiling crises?"

From the Tea Party:
"There, you see! Our GOP colleagues' constant bickering and blaming us
For insisting they adhere to their "No New Taxes Pledge to America" is what
Brought us to S & P's lowering of America's credit rating! We do not have to
Get our polarized act together or subscribe to partisan efforts to confront debt ceiling
Crises! All we need to do is to bad mouth all Republican legislators who do not
Agree with our carefully-structured political diatribes!"

From the President Barack Obama White House:
"There, you see! This is all S & P's fault! Why do they have to be so picky and
Judgmental, when evaluating the US debt ceiling crisis on the basis of the US Congress'
Constant bickering with one another? It's so unfair! So, Congress cannot always get
Along. Is that any reason to Downgrade the US' credit rating? I mean, can't S & P see
That their new AA+ Rating is bad for this administration's credibility?"

From Standard and Poor's:
"There, you see? This is what we have been pointing to, all along."

୫୦୧୫

P.T. Barnum and Hamid Karzai

Circus owner and promoter, P.T. Barnum is credited with the
Clichéd statement: "There's a sucker born every minute."

Afghanistan President, Hamid Karzai has apparently taken
Mr. Barnum's famous catch-phrase to heart.

Mr. Karzai finagles billions of dollars in US aid to build his
Country's pathetic infrastructure; then "loses" it to the Taliban.

Mr. Karzai blames the US for overhead drone strikes that mistakenly
Kill Afghan civilians; then praises America's military presence.

Mr. Karzai changes his opinion of America's military presence with
Whatever disgruntled mood he happens to be in.

Mr. Karzai blames the US for brutal Afghan warlords which assail his
Country; rather than burning the warlords' heroin poppy fields, as promised.

And so, regarding P.T. Barnum's iconic cliché:
"There's a sucker born every minute."

America is the poor "sucker," who has gotten into bed with a lawless
Middle Eastern country where conquering nations go to die.

Of course, America was duped into being an Afghan "sucker" by the
Biggest "sucker" of them all—US President George W. Bush.

Oh and as to Mr. Karzai—he might do well to keep in mind that he
And his "government" would not last one day, without a continuing
US military presence in place.

Who's the "sucker," now, Hamid?

৪৩

Lead by Example

In an affluent, white suburb of rural Mississippi, a group of Caucasian
Teenage youths participated in an underage drinking party. Two of
The young men, upon becoming sufficiently inebriated, promptly
Decided that they wanted to assault an African-American. It did not
Matter who it was—they simply wanted to wreak havoc and violence
Upon an individual with black skin.

The two young men, eighteen year-olds Deryl Dedmon and John Aaron
Rice, went out driving while intoxicated, looking for a vicious fight.
They found that fight in forty-nine year-old James Anderson, an
African-American man innocently standing beside his car within an
Interstate motel's camera-monitored parking lot. Several witnesses state
Dedmon and Rice parked in the lot, taunting Anderson with sneering
Racial slurs and epithets.

But Dedmon and Rice did not stop at words—they escalated into a
Savage beating of Anderson that left him in a crumpled heap.
After their racist anger had been sated; both Caucasian young men
Retreated to their vehicles, with one of them (believed by witnesses to
Be Dedmon) raising their fist into the air, shouting: "White power!"
Both Dedmon and Rice then casually drove away—with their preening
White trash girlfriends by their sides.

As poor Mr. Anderson, dazed and beaten to a bloody pulp, careened
To his feet and stumbled away, Dedmon—who had been in the process
Of exiting the motel parking lot—caught a glimpse of him in his
Ford F-250's headlights. He (Dedmon) promptly backed up his vehicle,
Aimed it at Anderson, and jumped the street's curb to physically run
Him over, killing him instantly.

The entire beating, fist raising, and murderous vehicular hit-and-run was
Captured by area motel cameras. Both Dedmon and Rice claim they
Are not guilty of anything, even though Dedmon gleefully bragged
To Rice at a McDonald's just down the street that he had: "Run that
N-word over!" What causes this kind of pure hatred, one might wonder?
Why, it couldn't possibly be these young men's biased, affluent upbringing,
Or that ex-GOP Governor, Hayley Barbour freely advocated the adoption
Of Confederate license plates and celebrated dubious KKK reminiscent
"Citizen Councils," could it?

Of course not—why, everyone knows both Mr. Barbour and these young men's
Parents are the complete personification of racial tolerance.

❦❧

"We're sorry…"

We have all heard the disenfranchised, mechanical operator's voice admonishing:
"We're sorry—the number you have called has been disconnected or is no longer
In service," when we are unable to reach a designated telephone number. We
Hear similar platitudes, whenever cell phone service has been unceremoniously
Interrupted. It is annoying and frustrating, to lose cell phone service, yes?

Recently, the Police inside a California transit station deliberately cut all cell phone
Service to users anywhere inside and within a nearby radius, due to their efforts to
Prevent a planned protest against police brutality from taking place. Apparently,
The week prior to the cell phone "kill," an angry mob had gotten out-of-hand, over
A senseless police killing, resulting in property damage and physical injuries.

And so—in the interest of "protecting" law abiding citizens; the police made the
Decision to bar cell phone access in and around the busy transit station hub.
Excuse me, but do I have this correct? The police were "protecting" citizens, by
Cutting off their access to any and all emergency personnel?

The police officers' logic is highly blunted—eliminating all cell phone service, in
The sole interest of preventing a planned protest, is nothing short of incredibly stupid,
If not criminally ludicrous. And, by the way, how does this dubious reaction balance
With the US Constitution's "Freedom to assemble" clause? The second protest was
Totally peaceful. No one got out of line or even raised their voice.

But then, they did not have a working cell phone to project their voice into, did they?
Fortunately, no one in the transit station experienced any critical dilemmas, requiring
The use of their cell phones. In response to angry debate over the forced cell phone
Shutdown, a self-righteous conservative news reporter sarcastically observed:
"So no one had cell phone service—what did people do, before 911?"

I will tell her what they did; nine times out of ten, they died.

∞∞

iExxon

Recently, Steve Job's Apple Corporation and oil industry giant, Exxon-Mobil, ("Exxon" for short) have been fighting it out, over which company will occupy The number one position, in American business profitability.

Let's see—we have Apple, which produces a multitude of ultra-cool computer And electronic products, including but not limited to the iPhone; the iPad; and The iPod. And we have Exxon, which produces refined crude oil and Alternative energy sources.

Exxon is railed against, due to the fact that it consistently produces yearly Profits in the billions of dollars. Those who vilify them would do well to Consider that it takes billions of those same revenue dollars, to locate, produce, And refine oil from sources other than the volatile Middle East. Exxon is at the Forefront of generating American oil self-reliance. It is easy for disgruntled Persons to go after them—they react to Exxon without bothering to Take in the overall American energy "Big picture."

Granted—Exxon has had its share of problems; most notably with their drunken Captain of the Exxon Valdez super tanker, who singlehandedly ruined a large Portion of the Alaskan coastline, when he ran his ship aground, leaking vast Amounts of eco-system ravaging oil. In the years following that disgraceful Debacle; however, Exxon has kept America's lugubrious demand for oil satiated. People can snipe and point fingers at them all they want to; but where would Americans be without the gas they provide, to power their vehicles?

Apple is railed against, due to the fact that their PCs are a closed system, along with Their immensely frustrating copy protection on iTunes' video streaming. Those who Vilify them would do well to consider that Mr. Job's Macintosh PCs are his creation, And if he wants them to operate as a closed system; that is entirely within his rights. And if consumers do not like iTunes' video streaming copy restrictions, limiting A film or TV show to their computer; they may take it up with the FBI, which sets Copyrighted film material standards.

Which company will win out, in the end? I have to admit; iPods and iPads look, Sound, and represent much cooler than refined crude oil—although without Exxon, I wouldn't be able to drive my car to the Apple store.

ಬಿಂಬ

The (So-Called) Logic Behind Gitmo

I see absolutely no incoming threats from Al-Qaeda, regarding the infamous
Nigerian airplane bomber, housed within an ordinary maximum security Michigan
Penitentiary, from several Christmases ago. What I do see is the principle of
"War on Terror" prisoners being kept "out of sight, out of mind".

As long as these designated "Enemy Combatants" remain incarcerated on a leased
Piece of land at the end of an island nation already famous for brutalized torture;
The American conscience is placated. Bring the prisoners to US soil and have them
Brutally tortured; and it presents a dubious political and legal conundrum, which
Would not sit so well with the collective American psyche.

Do you see the argument I am presenting here—when "Enemy Combatants" are
Held at Guantanamo Bay, out of the sight and minds of the US populace;
They can be tortured or even killed and no one even thinks about it, because it is not
Happening on US ground. Bring these "Enemy Combatants" onto US soil; however,
And their regard immediately changes. What is considered commonplace abroad,
Would be considered unspeakable within America, proper.

In the Batman film, *The Dark Night*, the joker wanted to take the best of Gotham's
Citizens—the city's "white knight," Harvey Dent—and prove that he could be
Brought down to the level of brutal, uncaring depravity. What if, through the eager
Utilization of torture and the endless (often legally unsupported) incarceration of its
Global enemies, Al-Qaeda and the Taliban have done the same thing to America?

ಬಂಣ

A Game from "The Game"

In California, the rapper, Jayceon "The Game" Taylor faced criminal
Charges brought by the Compton Sherriff's Department, stemming from
What has been characterized as a "tweet" incident gone terribly wrong.
Apparently, "The Game" put out a tweet for a rap music internship to his
Hordes of ecstatic rap followers and would-be rap emulators.

What happened next is complete speculation on both sides of the legal fence:
The Compton Sherriff's Department says the rapper deliberately "tweeted"
The direct line to the Compton Sherriff's Department, resulting in a "flash mob,"
That tied up the police switchboard for hours. The Sherriff's Department goes
Even further, suggesting legitimate police calls were disrupted by the telephone
Melee of eager participants vying for the rap internship.

Rapper "The Game" says that his cell phone was "hacked" and that someone
Other than him deliberately listed the Compton Sherriff's Department as the
Contact number for the prospective rap music internship. In any case, when
The Sherriff's department contacted the rapper, requesting the "tweeted"
Number be deleted; "The Game" did so. (Granted, on the third department
Request). Which should have been case closed—yes?

But no—the Compton Sherriff's Department railed against "The Game,"
Blaming him for the entire telephone line meltdown, as though the rapper
Had deliberately set about to inconvenience their department. Among the
Charges they leveled at "The Game," were "maliciously disrupting or impeding
Communications over a public radio frequency"; "obstruction of justice";
Along with any further charges relating to "delaying a police officer from doing
Their job."

I am a bit confused here—how is the rapper "obstructing justice," by having
Either mistakenly or through someone hacking his Twitter account, listing the
Compton Sherriff's Department as a contact number? And all of this anger at
Tying up the police switchboard aside—this indicates that the predominantly
White Compton Sherriff's Department is so helpful to the predominantly
African-American community it services, right? Yes? Anyone?

If you would like a real-life scenario of what the Compton Sherriff's Department
Means to the greater Compton community, I suggest listening to the rap album:
"Straight Outta' Compton" by N.W.A.

৪৩

Oracle

Former US Secretary of Defense, Donald Rumsfeld has been all over the
Conservative pundit television airwaves, elaborating on why everything
US President Barack Obama has done is a complete farce, along with offering
Sage advice on how to militarily deal with Bashar Al-Assad and Syria.

And the US populace cares about what Rumsfeld has to say, because....?

Pardon me, but anyone interested in listening to any buffoonish thing
Mr. Rumsfeld wishes to impart might want to recall how he (Rumsfeld) stated:
"Freedom's untidy; and free people are free to make mistakes and commit
Crimes and do bad things. Stuff happens." (2001)

I'm certainly glad I have Mr. Rumsfeld to explain the concept of freedom to me;
Aren't you?

Or how about this little spoken-word gem:
"Death has a tendency to encourage a depressing view of war." (2001)

Yes, I suppose soldiers dying in Iraq and Afghanistan would be found depressing.

And let's not forget this final slice of wisdom and candor:
"I am not going to give you a number for it, because it's not my business,
To do intelligent work." (2005)

You are correct, Mr. Rumsfeld—it is not.

☙❧

Inner Loyalty

1980's British rock icons, Def Leppard, were faced with unimaginable tragedy:
Their drummer lost his arm in a horrific motor vehicle accident:
How did they (the band) respond?
By postponing the release of their future album and tour, and constructing a high-tech
Drum kit, geared specifically so that he might play the drums, once again, using
His feet, in addition to his one good arm.

1980's American rock icons, Journey, were faced with unimaginable tragedy:
Their lead singer, Steve Perry, who put the band on the rock music map and carried them
To the top of the Billboard® charts, became incapacitated, due to degenerative hip disease,
Just before a major 1990's reunion comeback tour was to commence:
How did they (the band) respond?
By going ahead with their album and tour, without their trademark lead singer,
Engaging the first replacement front man available, who could believably approximate
Mr. Perry's distinctive, award-winning voice.

Is it just me, or do these band loyalty schematics seem ironically skewed?

80C8

Jennifer C. Wolfe is a forty-six year-old writer, who grew up in Maplewood, Minnesota and studied fiction writing and poetry at Century College in White Bear Lake. Ms. Wolfe has five previous publishing credentials: a poem "If" included within the Century College (White Bear Lake, MN) Spring 2008 *Student Lounge* literary magazine, along with two poems "St. Patrick's Day" and "Roller Coaster," published within the online edition of *Scrambler Magazine*, Issue 39, June 2010, a poem "Flower Child" published within the online edition of *The Muse – An International Journal of Poetry*, Issue 1, Volume 1, June, 2011, a poem "The Beauty of the Rain" published within the online edition of *The Muse – An International Journal of Poetry*, Issue 2, Volume 2, June, 2012 and two poems "Old Friends" and "New Friends" published within the online edition of *The Muse – An International Journal of Poetry*, Issue 3, Volume 3, June, 2013. Ms. Wolfe is listed within the poetry Directory of Writers at the *Poets & Writers* online magazine.

Beginning in 2008, Ms. Wolfe formed a collaborative publishing bond with BlazeVox Books of New York, under the guidance and tutelage of editor, Geoffrey Gatza. Her publishing credentials with the press are five poetry manuscripts, *Kick the Stones: Everyday Hegemony, Empire, and Disillusionment* published as an eBook by BlazeVox Books, New York, October 2008, *Yukon Rumination: Great Fun for All in the Land of Sarah Palin's Joe Sixpack Alaska*, published as an eBook by BlazeVox Books, New York, June 2009, *Healing Optimism, and Polarization*, published as an eBook by BlazeVox Books, New York, February 2010, *Somewhere Over the Pachyderm Rainbow: Living in an Elephant Controlled 2010 Election Diorama*, published as a print book by BlazeVox Books, New York, May, 2011, and *Reflections of Hostile Revelries*, published as a print book by BlazeVox Books, New York, July, 2014.

Somewhere Over the Pachyderm Rainbow received literary acclaim as a 2011 Indie Lit nominee for poetry. *Reflections of Hostile Revelries* is Ms. Wolfe's second print publishing with BlazeVox Books.